[DESIGN]

WORKING WITH PAPERCLAY
AND OTHER ADDITIVES

Working with *Paperclay*
and other additives

Anne Lightwood

The Crowood Press

First published in 2000 by
The Crowood Press Ltd
Ramsbury, Marlborough
Wiltshire SN8 2HR

British Library Cataloguing-in-Publication Data
A catalogue record for this book is available from the
British Library.

ISBN 1 86126 337 6

·Photograph previous page: Supported bowl form by
Frederick Payne. Fibreglass tissue within porcelain
slip.

Dedication

For my non-potting potter's mate who has been with
me through thick and thin and – literally – fire for
more than forty years. But also for all the workshop
assistants, students, Saturday girls and potting
colleagues who have shared the discoveries and
added immeasurably to the fun.

Acknowledgements

I am indebted firstly to all the contributors whose
work is featured for their generous response with
information and images, as well as to those not
mentioned individually whose replies to my
questionnaires provided much useful information
throughout the book; also very greatly to Claire
Brown of Duncan of Jordanstone College of Art in
Dundee who devised and carried out all the tests
detailed in Chapter 6, and to Metrosales, Paper Clay
Products and Potclays who provided the materials for
her to do them; to Andrew Topliss from Metrosales
for information and advice in discussions by phone,
to Dr Ian Morrison of the Scottish Crop Research
Institute for his helpful comments in the section on
fibres in Chapter 4, and finally to John Caton for
compiling the index.

Photographic Acknowledgements

The photographs in this book were taken by the
artists themselves, and by the following
photographers: Jackson A. Baker, Mike Barlow, Alan
Bye, Diana Corbin, Fiona Duckett, Kate Dyer, Carola
Forsström, Victor France, Annika Grossen, Stephen
Harper, Jill Hicks, John Jamieson, William J.
Macaulay, David Mingot, Andrew Morris, Lisa
Prendergast, Andrew Sanderson, Uffe Schultz,
Hirano Terumi, Shannon Tofts.

Typefaces used: text and headings, ITC Giovanni;
chapter headings, ITC Tiepolo.

Typeset and designed by
D & N Publishing
Membury Business Park, Lambourn Woodlands
Hungerford, Berkshire.

Printed and bound by Craft Print, Singapore.

Contents

There is no art without life
There is no life without development
There is no development without change
There is no change without controversy
There is no controversy without revolution

Spanish/Mexican saying quoted by Jules Heller at a conference, 'Paper as Art', 1978

Introduction

A large part of this book will be about taking risks and exploring new territory. All artists take risks when they expose their ideas, emotions or feelings to what may be an indifferent or even hostile world that is not yet ready to hear what they are saying. It is in the nature of any artist to be ahead of the field, articulating by some means – whether through the written word, by music, or visually – feelings that may be hidden within each of us, but which many do not have the means to express with any degree of eloquence.

Art should not be dull, and an artist must have something to say. Just as importantly, the message must have some universal relevance otherwise it will not stand the test of time, and will be seen as merely fashion or technique, fun for the moment but easily forgettable. Not every idea is worth preserving.

Society needs creative people in all spheres if progress is to be made. Change is inevitable in the modern world, and the designer, the maker and the entrepreneur can all become agents of change. They devise, produce and sell the products made possible by technological advances or by changes in creative thought. They are aware of social change, and their work may even help to bring it about by altering attitudes or perceptions. Indeed, an optimist may believe that such innovation can lead to a greater understanding of, and an improvement in, the social structure.

'Can ceramics be art?' is a question that has been asked continually through the years. The critic Herbert Read, writing in his book *The Meaning of Art* in the thirties, said:

> Pottery is at once the simplest and the most difficult of all arts. It is simplest because it is the most elemental; it is the most difficult because it is the most abstract.

Contrary to many of his day, he did at least imply that pottery was considered as a serious art form. But however 'old hat' it may seem to those involved, the question is still being posed as frequently at the start of a new century as ever before. This is surprising considering the blurring of boundaries that has taken place between disciplines in recent years. Clay as a material has no intrinsic form of its own, and in the raw state, very little value. It can be worked in a great variety of ways, and it can also take on the appearance of many other materials – but materials in themselves do not make art, and neither do techniques, however skilled or sophisticated they may be. It has to be the ideas expressed in a work, or the spirit that imbues it, that give the work value. Moreover, each onlooker will come with their own agenda, so the same piece will mean different things to different people; and it is a measure of the value of a work that it should speak on many levels.

The language of clay is international, and so the feelings it evokes may be more easily understood than some other forms of expression. Those who use clay feel that it speaks, that it has a mind of its own, and that a satisfying piece will have 'life'. To be true to its spirit it is necessary to be in love with the material, rather than with the idea of being a ceramic artist.

Many of those working in ceramics today are unsure of their identity. They would describe themselves as artists using clay, rather than as potters, and indeed many also use other materials at different times, or combine other materials with clay. The crossing of

'Armour' by Sara Challinor, 1998. Paperclay sculpture, raku fired.

interdisciplinary boundaries seems to cause problems, which arise as much as a result of the attitude of others towards the work, as from the technical difficulties which need to be overcome. Objects which seem to fall between pottery and sculpture and which have no recognizable function, or that are not easily categorized, appear to discomfort the viewer, and a visual language which is not immediately understood may create confusion or even antagonism. We are so continuously surrounded by beguiling and instantly recognizable visual images from advertising, television, newspapers and magazines, that something which cannot be immediately identified is suspect, and may be rejected if the effort of comprehension is too great. Fred Gatley's work cuts across several disciplines, and he expresses the dilemma succinctly – and surely speaks for many – when he writes:

> I have often experienced a confused attitude to my work which has almost appeared to be hostility, or at the least a discomfort with my inter-disciplinary tendency. At times I have been made to feel like some sort of subversive. However, as far as I am concerned, that is their problem. I have always worked in this way, crossing from one area to another as I felt my work dictated.

Others also feel their work is similarly misunderstood, falling between ceramics and sculpture and not fitting neatly into either category.

To be a potter, or a ceramic artist, or whatever those featured in this book choose to call themselves, is to take even greater risks than most. For not only are they experimenting with many new materials, they are also using those materials to construct works in a different idiom and frequently on a differing scale from anything that has gone before. And as if that were not enough, they then subject the fruit of much thought and many hours or weeks of labour to the fire – which will literally make or break it. For every happy accident revealed in the kiln there are many more wasters, providing the grist for exploration for future archaeologists.

This book recounts the explorations made by some ceramicists working today. Most would describe themselves as being on a journey with no known destination, some young and just starting out, others having a longer experience; but all would still call themselves students, for the learning process is never complete.

Even a few years ago this book could not have been written because the work described was not being made, and the ideas inspiring such work were not thought appropriate for expressing in a ceramic medium. Furthermore it is a sobering thought that by the time of publication, many of the ideas and methods in this book may already have been overtaken by further developments. With the amazing speed of modern communications the rate of change is so quick that new ideas can circle the globe almost before there has been time to assimilate the previous ones. There is so much information available on every aspect of ceramics – from kilns and materials to ideas and philosophies – that it may seem that overload has been reached, with just too many choices to be made. Tastes change quickly, and ideas that used to take a generation to be absorbed and assimilated now alter rapidly, from year to year or even month to month.

However, artists often work in isolation and, because of this, many believe that they are the first, or maybe the only ones to have discovered a particular technique, say, or to have developed a theory, and it can come as a surprise to find others working in a similar way far off in other parts of the world. The information may be around, but it may not be easy to find because it is so scattered, appearing in short magazine articles or as odd references in other publications. Of course the Internet is changing all that, but there

is still a place for a book which can be dipped into at leisure or used as a reference to check a specific piece of information.

The main purpose of this book is to assemble a selection of ideas and methods drawn from the knowledge and experiences of potters in using new materials such as paperclay, showing where they agree and where they differ. Also, by illustrating some of the thought-provoking work being produced, and by sharing recipes and methods, it hopes to encourage others to make their own discoveries. In gathering information a writer is dependent on the co-operation and interest of artists whose time is very precious, but who are nevertheless willing to spend it in explaining their working methods and ideas. With such a huge – and escalating – number of pottery books now available on the booksellers' shelves it is hard to remember the days, not so very long ago, when Bernard Leach's *A Potter's Book* or Dora Billington's *The Techniques of Pottery* were all that were available. Now, established artists are continually approached with requests for information or (very expensive) photographs by would-be authors or students writing dissertations. That is one reason why there has been an attempt to discover and illustrate the work of younger, less publicized artists alongside some who are already well documented.

For me, one of the most humbling aspects of researching the work of others has been discovering the yawning gaps in my own knowledge and understanding, and realizing how far there is still to go and how much

Bundle (two-chair sphere swan) by Graham Hay, 1998. Earthenware paperclay, height 50 × width 37 × depth 20cm (20 × 14.5 × 8in). Photo Victor France.

more there is to learn. The generosity of those who have opened their hearts and minds to expose their ideas and share their expertise is staggering, and the willingness of potters to share information must be unique in the creative arts. It is truly enriching.

A book such as this can never be definitive; creativity moves on too fast. At best it can show something of the broad sweep that makes up the ceramics' spectrum, and the work that certain makers are producing at a particular time; perhaps it may give some insight as to why they are doing it; and maybe it will also explain some of the methods they are using to get the results they have imagined. Individuals will go to great lengths to realize their ideals, and the number of processes or techniques that this may entail is enormous – and their discoveries may help to eliminate pitfalls for others. Perhaps the explanation of new methods will also allow creative processes even freer rein.

1 New Ways of Thinking

Pottery has one of the longest known histories of any craft skill – stretching back long before other recorded data – and the shards and remnants of pots found in archaeological excavations have been an important means of extrapolating information about the lifestyle and beliefs of other civilizations. Clay has also been used as a way to communicate, from Greek writing tablets in the centuries before Christ, to the glossy papers of today which incorporate quantities of china clay to give their smooth white surface.

Paper has a long history too, but as a material it is less likely to survive the dangers of damp and decay over so long a period. Paper made from papyrus has been found in the tombs of the Pharaohs in Egypt, and papermaking was a well developed skill in China in the time of Marco Polo, described by him in his accounts of his travels there in the thirteenth century. In Europe at that time vellum and parchment were used for writing on, and paper was a scarce commodity – though not many people could read or write.

In recent years, changes have taken place which alter our perceptions of both materials. Modern technology has made paper ubiquitous and very cheap: it is produced in vast quantities, from a whole variety of ingredients, in a huge range of qualities and finishes, and is frequently recycled, to be used over and over again in different guises. And almost because technology is so efficient – but also because it is so greedy of resources – papermakers have tired of bland, mass-produced materials, and have returned to handmaking methods using small quantities of interesting or unusual fibres. The character of the paper is considered by them to be as important as the marks made on it by pencil, brush or print, and indeed may be responsible for determining the nature of those marks.

Pottery, too, has moved from being mainly functional – whether for domestic

'Implements' by Carol Farrow, 1980s. Large-scale work in handmade paper, cast in situ, then painted and waxed. 1.5 × 1.5m (5 × 5ft). Photo Stephen Harper.

or ritual use – to being an art form, one in which artists have deliberately decided upon clay as their chosen medium. We no longer need items made from clay for utilitarian use in farm or kitchen or dairy; in many cases plastics or other materials have taken over, and while they may not have the aesthetic appeal of clay, they are often well suited to their purpose by being light, flexible and not easily broken.

Historically, ceramics have frequently been considered from a technical standpoint rather than an artistic one, though now the emphasis may have changed: in the words of Peter Lane, a noted British potter and writer, 'To occupy space while delighting the eye' is the concern of many. The awakening of imagination, the presentation of new ideas or the arousal of emotion have as valid a function to many ceramicists today as does the creation of a vase which holds water, or a jug that pours without dripping, to the potter working in a traditional way. The association with the wheel-thrown vessel may have been broken, but the legacy of function remains in work still described with utilitarian names such as teapot or jug; however, these vessels are made never to be used, but to be regarded primarily as objects of interest or beauty. When a pot is good, that matters more than its usefulness: its quality is sufficient function.

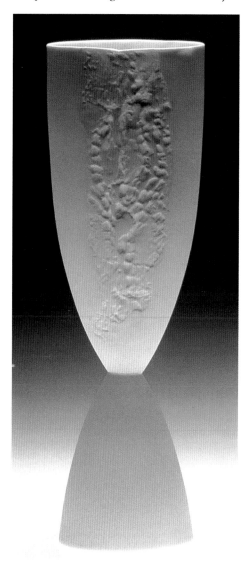

'Flute' by Angela Mellor, 1997. Bone china with paperclay inclusions. 18.5cm (7in) high.

Potters, like all other artists, are constantly looking for new freedom and means of expression, and are always searching for new materials or techniques with which to push the boundaries further. Clay is a wonderful material: infinitely variable, it can be everything, from an unfired adobe housebrick to the most delicate translucent porcelain. It has a life of its own, and potters feel this quality and respond to it. Clay does not remain the same for any length of time: beginning as a soft, malleable mass, it stiffens to a leather-hard state in which it can be carved or burnished; it shrinks as it dries; it changes state as it goes through the fire, perhaps many times; and very often it ends up as hard and long-lasting as the rocks from which it once decomposed.

Because so many processes are involved, and because there are so many things which can go wrong at every stage, potters have often been accused of being excessively concerned with materials and techniques, at the expense of an aesthetic awareness: they have asked 'How?' rather than 'Why?' And indeed, there is a danger that the potter becomes so caught up in the technical processes that the artistic content is forgotten or takes second place – but this is understandable when the product of many hours and much labour is literally put to the fire and could be lost forever. So, while 'wrong turnings can lead to great discoveries', to quote contemporary American ceramicist Kathy Triplett, conversely the fear of failure can act as a block to creativity.

It is hard to balance chance and control: too tight a control may stifle the chance development, too little may lead to chaos and collapse. But when one's livelihood, and perhaps also the welfare of others, depends on a successful firing resulting in a kilnload of pots for sale, the instinct to stick to a known and safe formula is understandable. All the more credit, then, to pioneers such as Picolpasso in Italy in the sixteenth century who literally burned his furniture and garden fence in his desperate attempts to keep his kiln going to reach the desired high temperature; or to Josiah Wedgwood and his peers whose meticulous records over many years included numerous failures but also led to such spectacular advances in materials and techniques that many of his discoveries are still being used today. And now paperclay comes in.

'*Listing*' by Lorraine Fernie, 1999. Porcelain paperclay with acrylic colour, once-fired to 1260°C. 55 × 28cm (22 × 11in).

New Freedoms

While researching for this book, one maker after another has given as their reason for changing to paperclay the fact that because it is so easy to use, it frees the mind and so allows the imagination to take over. Thereafter the resulting work is much more likely to survive the processes of drying out and the hazards of the kiln. Ideas are often inspired by, or at least taken further during the process of making. Not all ideas will be good, and sorting those of real value from the bad or merely expedient takes experience as well as stern judgement: but many potters feel that paperclay allows them to be more of an artist and less of a technician.

The increasing number of arts courses now available in colleges worldwide, and the freedom within these courses to experience a variety of different disciplines, materials and techniques, means that the emerging artist has available a range of possibilities that those of earlier generations must envy. Perhaps it is for this reason that many users of paperclay are young people, recently graduated, and free from the 'mug and jug' ideologies previously prevalent, particularly in Britain. The old-fashioned image of the potter as a rural craftsman – perhaps not very well educated or imaginative, and turning out large quantities of wares to be sold in local markets – has long since gone.

In its place is a college graduate, possibly with some knowledge of the basic elements of several disciplines, willing to cross boundaries and embrace new techniques, frequently urban, just as often female, and with an international perspective on the world. Their main income is more likely to be earned from teaching than from selling their work. Many now expect to exhibit their work in galleries as art objects, considered for their intellectual content, rather than selling them in markets or craftshops where function may be the first consideration.

Fluid Thought

Some time ago at a potters' conference Brian Gartside was demonstrating the making of paperclay for the first time in Britain, and graphically demonstrated what he described as 'fluid thought' – the sort of imaginative lateral thinking that motivates many artists today. He put several lumps of clay into a bucket of water: although they would gradually dissolve, it was still possible to pull them out again, to count them separately, and to handle each one. But when several cups of water were put into a bucket there was no way in which the separate cupfuls could then be isolated or identified; if the water were then to be poured out over the ground it would percolate through whatever it touched, flowing over or around objects in its path. Brian suggested that water symbolizes creative thought and that similar free-flowing processes

'Curve/Cove' by Tony Franks, 1999. Vitreous bone china with leaves and seaweed, extruded bone china pellets, fired to 1200°C, ground and sandblasted, coloured with vanadium pentoxide and titanium mix, underglaze stains and copper sulphate, fired to 1220°C. 43 × 37 × 23cm (17 × 14.5 × 9in). Photo Shannon Tofts.

could be applied to making methods. By asking 'what are the basics?' we should look afresh at what we do. He suggested water might be the most important element in claymaking, both physically and symbolically.

Several years later at a similar conference, Alan Watt, a lecturer from Australia, showed how far this process had already gone. As an exercise, a group of students were each given one kilo of clay and told to stretch it as far as it could go, by whatever means they could think of. Some coiled it into long strips, some rolled it out into thin sheets, others threw it, or patted it into small pebbles which covered a large area – but the overwhelming winner was the one who mixed the clay into a bucket of water and poured the resulting slip into the river close to where it entered the sea!

In spite of producing many ceramicists of international stature, Britain has been slower than some countries – notably Australia and America – to break away from the type of classicism espoused by great proponents such as Bernard Leach, and to absorb abstract work by Peter Voulkos or others like him. For many years West Coast America was a long way away, in tastes as well as geography. Norway does not have a long ceramic tradition, and students at the National College of Art and Design in Oslo are challenged to think of ceramics as a medium for creating art equal to any other. Words with a specific connotation such as 'cup' or 'pot' are not used, glazes may be called 'colours which melt', while slips are described as 'non-melting surfaces'. Certainly this approach gives freedom of thought, but it is essential that it is also combined with technical skill and high quality design and drawing.

The Need for Skills

While some may feel that ceramic art should break free from the inheritance of domestic ware – 'the tyranny of repetition' as it has been described – and be imbued with a greater spiritual content, it is important that the emphasis given to concept does not overwhelm that of learning a skill. To have gained skill in any medium implies a process in which it takes time both to understand the material and to master the discipline imposed by it. To have mastered a skill is not to narrow the options, but to be empowered with the confidence that such knowledge can give.

The difficulty for many today is that skills have traditionally been associated with *craft* ideas rather than with artistic concepts, and craft skills are often seen as purely manual and technological. It also takes a long time to acquire a skill such as throwing a well-balanced pot, while other techniques such as casting or handbuilding may appear to give results more quickly. However, no matter what technique is employed, it must be seen as a means to an end rather than as an end in itself.

While many of the following chapters will describe work that is difficult to categorize, it is by no means the intention to belittle in any way the work of those who choose to remain within traditional boundaries, or to imply that the pieces they produce are somehow of less value because they are meant to be used. Our daily lives are immeasurably enriched by being surrounded by objects which combine function as well as beauty. A table on which food is presented on handmade dishes is a sure way to rouse the appetite – and if objects can also provide food for thought, so much the better. But much has already been written on traditional skills, methods and materials, and they are not the subject of this book.

*'*C*urved Information as Object' by Graham Hay, 1998. Four tons of government documents, installed in the High Court of Australia during the National Sculpture Forum. 2.5 × 2.5 × 6m (8 × 8 × 20ft). Photo Marcia Lochhead.*

Until now, the material of ceramics has always been considered to be clay – 'ceramics' comes from the Greek word 'keramos', meaning clay – and the most important technique to be fire, but perceptions are changing so that clay may be only one ingredient in a mix of materials used, and fire is not always a necessity. Paperclay, even when it is paper thin, has amazing unfired strength and can be handled easily because it is so light and because it retains flexibility. Very thin sheets actually have more resilience and are more easily handled *before* firing; in fact it is not unknown for unfired pieces to be created for site-specific exhibitions and treated with acrylic paints, rather than glazed – and they are then dismantled at the end of the show and the materials recycled for further use. Sometimes installations are left *in situ* outdoors, the wind and the weather gradually dissolving them back into the earth, in the same way that sculptors such as Andy Goldsworthy build from such transitory materials as leaves or frozen snow; photographs are all that ultimately remain. Since a kiln is no longer essential, some artists work publicly on site, frequently creating pieces with the involvement of their audience.

There are now many ceramic conferences, with demonstrations, lectures and discussions taking place all over the world. At these, internationally known ceramicists can share their expertise with students, practising potters and interested amateurs, and widely differing ideas can be disseminated along with hands-on experience. The results of possibly years of trial and error are distilled down to a brief presentation. Ceramics are becoming performance art – but still the difficulty remains as to how to describe the objects that are made.

2 The Composition of Clays

As Old as the Hills

To understand how different the qualities of paperclay are from most normal clay bodies, it is necessary to know a little about the origins of clay, and the infinite variety of clays to be found in almost every part of the world. Clay is almost as old as the hills. It is created by the decomposition of rocks which have been thrust up by the action of volcanoes to form mountains. Gradual weathering by rain and frost wears away the rock, breaking it into pieces which are then borne by rivers and floods far from the starting point, leaving some en route and gathering other materials as the flow continues. Such a process is long term and continuous.

If a piece of rock such as granite is broken apart it will show traces of several different components that can be seen easily: mica which glitters, quartz which

Earthenware piece by Roy Ashmore, 1999. Mixed clays. 60 × 40cm (24 × 16in).

*F*our pieces, stacked
by Liz Cave, 1998.
Layers of different clays
mixed with stains and
other additions.

is hard, or feldspar which gradually decomposes to form kaolin when soluble salts eventually wash away. The alumina and silica in these compounds gradually combine with water to form clay, and as it is transported along rivers the particles become graded, with the coarsest and heaviest settling first. The grinding effect of the stones on the river bed and the continuous influence of the water act like a ball mill, so that as clay is carried further from its source the size of the particles becomes steadily smaller; but other detritus, most visibly iron, is picked up as well.

Clay particles are composed from many minute clay crystals which bond together and are lubricated with water, making the clay plastic. The crystals are flat and roughly hexagonal in shape; they slide over each other in a sort of lattice-like formation and, as the clay dries out, the particles bind more closely together so that the clay shrinks. Fractals are the figures or surfaces produced by repeated division and subdivision of polygonal forms; this is what happens when hard clay slakes to slurry. They have been described as 'the patterns of chaos', and 'order from chaos' is one of the ways in which many potters describe their motivation.

Primary clays are those that have remained close to their starting point. They are much purer, such as kaolin or china clay, the main ingredient of porcelain, which is found in relatively few places in the world. Primary clays tend to have a larger particle size, and to be less plastic.

Secondary clays are rarely so pure, and deposits are often found far away from the place of origin. Many additions and impurities are picked up along the way, most often iron or other oxides, and these affect the colour of the clay. The size of the particles is also much smaller, and secondary clays are usually plastic.

As clay sediments settle they form into layers, and other materials are trapped within these layers so that the clays formed vary in content or texture; even a single clay bed will probably not be uniform, and may contain strata consisting of several different types of clay. Organic vegetable matter will decompose, and sedimentary clays frequently contain carbon from this, making the body acidic. This is a useful characteristic in the souring and storage of clay, as the acidity polarizes the particles, causing them to attract each other and thus increase plasticity.

The Plasticity of Clay

Generally speaking, weathering increases the plasticity of clay. Frost breaks up large lumps into smaller pieces, and rain washes away soluble salts. The smaller the particle size the more plastic the clay, although too great a proportion of very fine particles in a clay body can cause it to collapse during the making process. Clay needs to have a variety of particle sizes, both flat platelets and larger granules, and different clays are therefore frequently blended to produce the desired qualities. Once mixed, the clay can be stored for long periods providing it is kept damp, and it will improve as the water content evens out throughout the mass. Thus, in the same way that well-born fathers in Britain would lay down a cellar of port for their sons – bottles which would not be drunk for many years, or even in their own lifetime – so it is said that Chinese potters laid down clay pits so that their sons or grandsons would inherit a good legacy and be able to carry on the potting dynasty. Marco Polo, the first Western traveller to penetrate into China, described:

> … clay which is dug as though from a mine and stacked in huge mounds, then left for thirty or forty years … you must understand that when a man makes a mound of this earth he does so for his children.

Michael Cardew, a pioneer British potter, recounts how he left his pottery at Wenford Bridge during the Second World War, and, because he then worked in Africa for some years afterwards, did not return for far longer than he had intended. He found the clay, which had been dug and stored in a damp dark cellar before his departure, in absolutely perfect condition and ready to be wedged for use.

This is one area where paperclay does not follow normal clay behaviour.

The Characteristics of Paperclay

Because paperclay contains a high proportion of vegetable material, if it is stored for a long time this natural fibre, whatever it is, will always start to rot, and this process of decomposition will cause the clay to smell. More importantly it may also produce moulds, the spores of which can be injurious to health. The safest way to store paperclay for any lengthy period is dry, either as sheets or as blocks; these can then be soaked down in water when required for use. This is undoubtably one of paperclay's most useful attributes.

The cellulose in the fibre can be likened to a series of minute hollow tubes: these act like tiny drinking straws, sucking the water deep into the core of the clay without damaging the structure of the body as a whole. This is why bone-dry sheets of paperclay can be bonded after only wetting the edges, and why wet paperclay can be added to dry pieces without cracking, or even why wet paperclay slip can be applied to a piece which has already been bisque fired. This amazing property is one which contemporary potters and sculptors take advantage of and use to the full.

But it is also one of the reasons why paperclay is not, in general, a suitable body either for domestic ware or for thrown work, unless the piece is thrown quite rapidly and kept relatively thick. This is because, with paperclay, the water used to lubricate the ball of clay while throwing is drawn deep into the structure of the piece, instead of remaining on the surface as normally happens, and this can cause the form to collapse quite suddenly into a soggy mass as the walls are pulled up thinner. Sometimes cylinders thrown from paperclay are used to make an armature or as a support for large sculptural work, but the fibres in the clay mix make it difficult to turn or trim satisfactorily, and tools become blunted quite quickly.

The very finely milled cellulose now being manufactured by some suppliers may prove the exception to the throwing rule, since a very small quantity well dispersed throughout the clay can improve its handling characteristics without damaging its plasticity. But throwing is a fast, repetitive method requiring large quantities of clay, and there is really little advantage in making paperclay for it when so many suitable bodies already exist. This is why there is little domestic ware shown in the book, and why very few pieces are round.

It is also usually unsatisfactory to pug paperclay, since the fibres tend to clog up within the barrel unless the pugmill is a large industrial type. Extruding is difficult for the same reason, though some of the very finely milled fibres may be suitable for this, while homemade pulp is not.

Vessel by Lizzie Rice. Detail showing the vitality of the hand-built surface; white stoneware paperclay with coloured inserts.

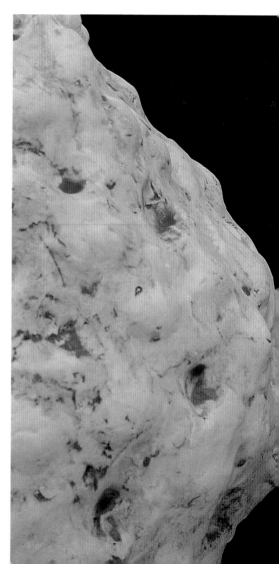

As Common as Mud?

The ingredients that combine to form clay are found in about 60 per cent of the land mass of the earth and are therefore extremely common. Today, however, few clays are used by studio potters straight from the ground 'as dug' – the description which years ago used to appear in manufacturers' lists, at the beginning of my potting experience. In fact there are now so many types of clay – prepared to suit every possible use, described in accurately detailed and enticing full colour catalogues, neatly wrapped and labelled and ready to use straight from the bag – that it is a wonder anyone wants anything more, or still bothers to make their own.

Strictly speaking, the description 'clay' refers to a single material from one source. When clays of differing types from varied sources are mixed to create a composite material, this is described as a clay 'body': most of the clays used by studio potters today are therefore 'bodies'. In previous generations this was not always the case, and potteries were frequently set up near a good local supply of clay. The type of clay dictated the sort of ware which could be made, and additions such as ground shards of previously fired clay might be added to open up the clay for use as bricks or for large pieces, or a finer slip of a lighter colour might be sieved in order to coat the surface of some domestic ware with a smoother surface.

For many potters the excitement of taking common, ubiquitous, cheap ingredients and converting them into something personal – something that contains, as it were, their own handwriting, a material from which long-lasting objects of function, beauty and imagination can be produced – is one of the chief attractions of working with clay. Time and time again when speaking to potters, and even more to artists who have turned to clay after using other materials, the *vitality* of clay is mentioned – the feeling that it comes alive under one's fingers, gaining a life and character of its own, and even suggesting the way in which a form might develop.

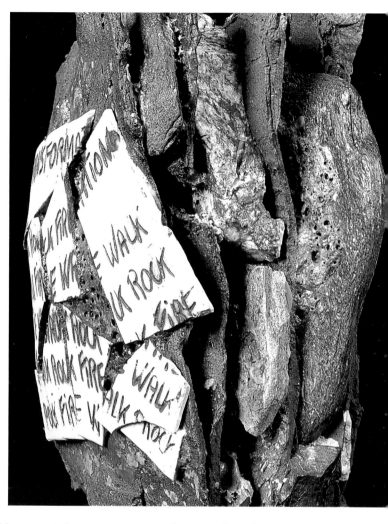

'Land/Book/Land' by Lotte Glob. Mixed clays with rock inclusions, showing the reaction of one with another.

Clay Components

Obviously with so many types of clay, and because it has so many uses, there can be no one recipe for a successful body. But certain elements are as necessary for a fine porcelain as for a sturdy brick clay, however much the proportions or actual materials may vary.

The first is a *filler* which forms the main bulk of the body. It may be a local clay, as it is still in many parts of the world; or it may be a refined powder from the manufacturer. Its nature will determine the firing temperature and very likely also the colour.

The filler clay may need the addition of a *plasticizer* to make it more workable. This could be a ball clay with finer particles, or bentonite which has very tiny platelets and only needs to be added in small quantities. Alternatively a very fine, smooth clay might need the addition of an *opener* such as fireclay, sand or grog to give it texture and make it suitable for a particular use. Quartz is sometimes also used for this.

The fourth element is a *vitrifier*, a material containing silica, that will melt within the body thus fusing the whole together in a permanent, non-reversible bond. Feldspars, nepheline syenite, whiting or talc may be used, depending on the temperature to which the clay is to be fired.

Tip
If large quantities of slip are to be made from plastic rather than powdered clay it is easiest to cut the clay into slices, allow them to dry out till hard, then put the pieces into a stout plastic bag and break them up by beating with a mallet until the clay crumbles into smallish lumps, after which it can quite easily be added to water and mixed until it is all absorbed and smooth.

Weighing dry clay will give a more accurate record of the amount needed for future batches than will weighing plastic clay, where the water content may vary.

The materials used, and the proportion in which they are combined, determine the type of clay body created, but all will contain those four components to some degree or another. Many potters in the developed world who are using clay as an artistic means of expression in the studio, will not start from raw materials but will combine differing quantities of several manufactured clays to achieve the type of body they want. Similarly, traditional village potters will mix clays and add straw or grasses or sandy material to make the local clay suitable for the job in hand; the work made is usually appropriate for the local clays, and made to satisfy the definite needs of the community. In Bophuthatswana, for instance, fine sand from anthills is used as an additive, along with ash or dried cow dung, and the mud-built kilns are fired with anything that will burn, including fruit peel, corn husks and sawdust. Such firings are unlikely to reach a very high temperature, though the intensity of the flame as it flares in certain areas may be extreme and put great stress on the clay body. In India, while men will throw or form using press moulds, handbuilding is seen as women's work, and coiling is the method used for making the ubiquitous tandoori ovens. These are about 1m (3ft) high and have to withstand uneven heating and cooling, as firing and cooking take place simultaneously. The fuel is burned on the bottom, nan bread or chappatis are slapped on the side walls, and other food is cooked on skewers at the top. The clay that is used incorporates dry, powdered cow dung and is formed into thick coils for building. The dung serves two important purposes: it opens out the clay body, making it less liable to thermal shock; and it also makes use of a common substance to bulk out the more valuable clay so that less of that material is needed. Because the dung is dry it is relatively easy to powder finely and blend evenly throughout the mixture, and its use means that the firing temperature of the body can be lower – another economy. In many areas any natural product, such as hair, paddy waste, rice husk, coconut fibre, grass or leaves, is likely to be added to the terracotta clay so that it goes further, and to make it easier to handle in the raw state; however, if too great a proportion is used, the material will risk becoming very light and friable, and too full of air spaces after firing. In India there is still a tradition of making large numbers of votive pieces to be used with offerings at festivals. Frequently these are not fired, but are painted or stained with brilliantly coloured dyes and left at shrines to decay gradually and return to nature; alternatively they are put into water or floated down the river, in which case their dissolution and disappearance will be a deliberately chosen part of their existence.

Clays for Different Purposes

Adobe Bricks

In many of the drier areas of the world, adobe bricks are the normal building material and structures built with them last for many years, providing they are maintained regularly, particularly after rainfall. The bricks are built from the local clay with the addition of chopped straw and, depending on the type of clay, also sand. If it is available,

'Green Wood Kiln' by Hannah Ayre, 1997. Beechwood framework with local clay.

Fire flower kilns by Wali Hawes, built using an adobe brick construction, and looking remarkably similar to many traditional ovens and grain stores.

cement may be added for a really strong blend. The proportions might be four to five parts of clay, with two to four parts sand and one of cement mixed with straw and water to bind. Sometimes the clay content may be as little as 40 per cent. These bricks are sun dried and are not fired.

Israeli Experiences

Some years ago at a meeting of the International Academy of Ceramics, Professor Ogen of the Ceramics Department of the Bezalel Academy in Jerusalem presented a paper describing experiments that had been carried out to test simple methods of making cheap, strong building materials from easily sourced local clays. Israel has a history of earth houses dating back hundreds of years, and in some areas the traditional clay ovens known as taboons are still in use. Like the tandoori oven, a taboon is made from earth mixed with donkey dung, and through use and the heat of baking becomes hard and rain resistant. The taboon is built up by pinching, and is uniformly thin-walled, no more than 2cm (¾in) thick. It is circular, tapering to a closed curve like the pointed end of an egg. It is thought that the dung contains a natural 'glue' which helps the binding process, and the straw fibres, having been digested, are much finer than the chopped straw used in adobe blocks.

The aim was to find an earth/fibre combination that would be rain resistant, and would also have a reliable mechanical strength. Tests were carried out with mixtures containing straw and sawdust and with nylon fibres, plus the addition of phosphates and sodium silicate. Phosphoric acid reacted with carbonates in the clay causing bubbling, but it was found that 5 per cent each of mono-aluminium phosphate and sodium silicate added to a local red clay called terra rosa significantly increased strength while at the same time reducing the firing temperature needed. This produced a stable material comparable to other building blocks, yet one which was considerably cheaper. The colour and texture of the blocks harmonized naturally with the landscape, making the material suitable for use in stabilizing field terraces or for other topographical uses. The phosphoric acid had the effect of hardening the clay very quickly so that only one day's supply was made at a time; it is also caustic until mixed with the clay when it neutralizes, so gloves were worn when handling it. The bricks that were made were fired on site in a simple kiln, the outside layer of the brick stack acting as the kiln wall, a method still commonly used in Egypt and elsewhere.

Raku Bodies

Clay for quick, low-temperature firings such as raku or pit-firing, needs to contain a high proportion of grog, sand or some other opener so that it will withstand the thermal shock of sudden heating and cooling; but once this has been added, most clays from porcelain to fireclay can be used safely.

In Thailand the local clay is dug, slaked down and then mixed with 'grog'. The grog is a clay slip mixed with rice husks to form pats which are dried out in the sun. The pats are then burned, using the husks contained in them as the only fuel, and the resulting material is sieved. Clay and grog are then mixed and pugged to form the body from which flameproof cookware or porous water containers are made.

Firing these takes only an amazing 15 minutes. First a layer of rice straw is laid down, followed by bark, then the pots are laid on this on their sides, with more bark placed in between them and big bundles of rice straw piled all over the top. More bundles are added as required until the desired temperature has been reached.

'Pressed Form' by Zoe Hall, in layered terracotta paperclay.

Earthenware Clays

Earthenware clays are secondary clays, usually of a fine particle size and therefore very plastic. Historically they were in most common use since their deposits are widespread and their firing temperature need not be high, usually no more than 1100°C, though it is frequently less than this. Some can be taken higher, reaching almost 1200°C. Earthenware clays are sometimes light in colour, but are frequently stained with iron or other oxides which colours them from cream to a warm rust – terracotta – when fired. The higher the temperature at which these clays are fired, the deeper will be the colour until it becomes dark brown; if taken too high it will melt. Potters make use of this in glazes that are taken to a higher temperature, where some earthenware clay may be added to give colour or character to a stoneware glaze. At lower temperatures an earthenware piece is still porous and will need a glaze firing or further treatment if it is to be waterproof. In hot countries potters make use of this porosity in water containers, since the evaporation of some of the water has a cooling effect. Indian 'summer pots' for storing water are specially made with clay containing larger particles of rice or wheat husk that leave the clay more porous, thus cooling the water even more; those for winter are made with a different clay body.

In Majorca, as in other regions of Spain, cooking dishes are made to be used directly on the top of the stove in contact with the flame, and many would argue that the type

of dish is crucial to the flavour of the food, giving it a particular quality. A sandy, open clay is used which is never fired above 950°C, sometimes even lower, and this causes the ware to give a dull sound when tapped. The underfiring prevents any chance of vitrification and keeps the open structure of the clay. Flat pieces have a surprisingly thin base which is turned to a very shallow convex curve. The sides are usually straight, and only the inside is glazed. These factors would not appear to add up to making a strong piece, yet the ware is surprisingly robust and it builds up a glossy patina with use.

Stoneware

Stoneware temperatures are reached when the body is vitrified, usually above 1200°C, though most potters would fire higher than this, to 1260–80°C or above. Although glaze is often used decoratively, strictly speaking it is not necessary because a degree of vitrification will have taken place within the body of the piece, making it no longer porous. As its name implies, stoneware is harder than earthenware and the colour range tends to be softer. At this temperature the bond between clay body and glaze is tight, the outer glaze surface fused closely with the structure of the clay, making the fit of the glaze and body crucial. If the glaze contracts more than the underlying clay body the glaze will crack or craze in a network of fine lines. (This characteristic is used deliberately in raku glazes where crazing may be encouraged, and the web of lines emphasized by smoking.) If the contraction of the body is greater than that of the glaze covering it, the coating of glaze will be compressed outwards from the surface, resulting in spitting or spalling, with areas of glaze being pushed off in extreme cases. Ideally the glaze should be in just enough compression to remain craze free.

Wall fragment by Hazel Thomson. Laminated structure with porcelain casting slip and paper.

Porcelain

The word 'porcelain' is taken from the Italian *porcelino* meaning 'little pig', and was so named because its translucency and pearly surfaces resembled the cowrie shells which were shaped like a little pig and were sometimes used as currency. It is a pure white primary clay which is relatively non-plastic with a large particle size, and consists chiefly of kaolin which has been described as the 'bones' of the clay, with feldspar forming the 'flesh'. Early oriental porcelain ware first arrived in Europe during the sixteenth century as ballast in East India ships bearing cargoes of spices, silk and tea; it had a bluish tinge from the petuntse it contained (the Chinese name for a type of feldspar similar to Cornish stone). European porcelain used alabaster as a flux, giving a more yellow tone. At high temperatures the silica from within the feldspar fluxes silica from the kaolin to form mullite 'needles' – long, square-sided crystals which interlace, stiffening the vitrified clay and giving strength to the finished piece. This is a characteristic of both stoneware and porcelain bodies.

Porcelain can be more difficult to work with than many clays, absorbing large quantities of water during throwing, then suddenly becoming soggy and collapsing unless this is done rapidly. In order to obtain translucency, its most special characteristic for many potters, it is often thrown more thickly than required, then turned away to achieve the desired fineness in the finished piece. This is a highly skilled technique which can result in a great number of seconds or kiln wasters. Conversely as a hand-building material porcelain will dry out rapidly, becoming brittle in a short working time. It is often fired at temperatures even higher than for stoneware, particularly when translucency is desired – to 1300°C or above, if both kiln and claywork can stand it. These are almost glass-forming temperatures, so the body undergoes tremendous stress and becomes completely vitrified. The danger is that the clay will slump and the piece become unpleasantly warped, though some potters have learned to control this, and to use it to good effect.

Bone China

Bone china might be described as a British version of porcelain. It came to its name when European potters in the eighteenth century were desperately trying to find the secret of the pure whiteness and translucency of the ware expensively imported from China. Many combinations of materials were attempted – with additions which included ground glass, sand and shells – until it was discovered that ground animal bones could give the desired whiteness and be used to develop a translucent white body. This is very short to work, and its fragility when dry makes it difficult to handle. Unusually, it is most often fired to a higher temperature in the bisque firing than in the glaze, and at this stage the ware is often supported in alumina or in setters to prevent warping. However, bone china is eminently suitable for use as a casting slip. This factor was an important discovery in the development and huge expansion of the English pottery industry. The increasingly fashionable pursuit of tea or chocolate drinking called for finer vessels than the earthenware or salt glaze formerly used in the coffee houses, and entrepreneurs, such as the two Josiahs – Spode and Wedgwood – spent much time and money in experiments to perfect a suitable new material.

3 Additives and their Effects

The many different additives used to alter the characteristics of clay bodies can be divided into three categories. The first might be called the *ingredients*, substances such as feldspar, flint or oxides which are blended with the original base clay to form a composite body, after that they cannot be separated or removed. Manufacturers, or individual potters making their own mix, include many different materials in their recipes in order to alter the handling, texture or firing range of a clay body to make it suitable for a particular purpose. These additions become part of the structure of the clay, blending within it in the raw state, and fusing in an irreversible process when fired.

The second group could be described as *inclusions*: molochite and grogs of all grades come into this group, as do coloured particles of fired clay aggregates, glass granules and sand. These are added to alter the texture, strength or finished appearance of the fired clay. Mostly they have already been calcined or fired, and therefore the effect on them of further action in the heat of the kiln is minimal. They act like building blocks within the clay, supporting the structure. Theoretically they could be sieved out of the clay again before firing, leaving the original clay unaltered.

Detail of 'Glenisla Spring' by Tony Franks, 1998. Press-moulded vitreous bone china with peat and ferns, fired to 1200°C, sandblasted outside. 35cm (14in) diameter × 25cm (10in) high. Photo Shannon Tofts.

The third group comprises *organic extras*: these are added to an existing clay body, and are included to alter the handling characteristics of the unfired body; sometimes, as is the case with paper, they also give additional green strength during making. They will ultimately burn away in the fire leaving only traces behind, or gaps in the structure where they once were. Materials such as paper, leaves or straw, as well as both natural and man-made fibres, come into this category. Seeds and grains of lentils or rice pressed into the surface can also be included, since they burn away but leave an impression of their former presence in the texture.

Ingredients

Ballclay

This is a generic name given to a variety of clays. These are secondary clays of a small particle size often forming the main bulk of the clay body. They are too slippery to be used on their own, but can have sand or grog added to them, or they may be added to other clays to give greater plasticity. Since they fire to a dense, hard body they are most often used in the stoneware range of temperatures. Ballclays are varied in composition, frequently appearing as dark grey or bluish in colour in the raw state due to carboniferous material which has been picked up in transit. This burns away in the kiln, so that ballclays are commonly light in colour when fired. They are likely to have a high shrinkage because of their small particle size; they may also act as a flux.

One explanation for the name 'ballclay' is that the clay was dug out of the pits in blocks weighing approximately 11 kg (25lb) known as balls; another is that it came from the balls of clay carried in pannier loads by donkeys along the narrow lanes in Devon and Dorset from the clay beds, where there were extensive, good quality deposits, to the coast where the clay was then loaded onto boats. At a time when roads were unpaved and vehicles horse-drawn, such a means of transport for a heavy, unwieldy cargo such as clay made very good economic sense. The clay also acted as ballast in boats bringing south commodities such as coal; the boats would otherwise have returned north empty. Even until the late nineteenth century this was the method used by the Heron potteries in Kirkcaldy in Scotland to obtain the high quality materials needed for what ultimately became their best known production, Wemyssware.

'Book page' by Lotte Glob. Mixed clays with porcelain inset; the dark clays have vitrified and started to bubble and melt, the colour bleeding into the porcelain. 35 × 29cm (14 × 11in).

China Clay: Kaolin

A primary clay, and on its own not very plastic because of its relatively large particle size; however, it is often a component in other prepared clays, and it is the main ingredient in porcelain. It fires white, and at high temperatures – around 1300°C – it becomes translucent. Its name derives from the Chinese word *kao-ling*, meaning 'the high mountains' (in China) where the first deposits were extracted; it is found in relatively few sites in the world. That, combined with the technical problems associated with both working and firing it to such high temperatures, has made it expensive and given it a precious reputation.

In her fascinating history of the development of porcelain, *The Arcanum*, Janet Gleeson describes how, throughout the eighteenth century in Europe, collecting porcelain became such a mania among kings and princes that it was as highly valued as gold, and the unfortunate potters working day and night to discover the secret of the pure whiteness of oriental porcelains were literally kept under guard as prisoners lest the secrets of the formulae (the arcanum) they were working on were divulged to rivals. In recent years, however, manufacturers have developed a whole range of porcelain bodies which are reliable and affordable, and, in combination with stains and colours, many more possibilities are now available to the studio potter.

Feldspars

A whole group of minerals which occur naturally as a component of clay; also used as an important ingredient in high temperature glazes. Feldspars contain alkalis, usually either soda or potash, the latter being the most common. They act as a flux in both body and glaze, and bond the clay particles together within the clay body.

Silica

Introduced into the body by adding flint or quartz in amounts of less than 25 per cent. This helps to prevent cracking and gives hard-fired strength.

Bentonite

A clay containing a high proportion of silica; it adds plasticity by varying the particle size within the body. However, it has a very high shrinkage which can cause cracking, so it is used in only very small amounts – around 2 to 3 per cent – to improve the workability of short clays, and slightly more in glazes where it helps the adherence of the glaze to the surface of the piece. This is particularly useful in raw glazing where bentonite may replace some of the china clay.

Tip
Bentonite has very tiny particles which expand enormously in water, so when adding bentonite to a mixture it should be gently blended dry by hand to disperse it through one of the other heavier ingredients (such as quartz) before adding both to the wet mix. If it is put straight into water it will form a sticky, spongy mass which is very difficult to break up and dissolve evenly.

Bentonite is used in large quantities in the oil industry where it is an important lubricant for drilling operations.

Fireclays

These are refractory clays with a high alumina content often found near coal measures, and used for making firebricks, drainpipes and building bricks; they are also an ingredient in most stoneware clays. They are hard to break down and need milling to make them workable. Generally they have a coarse particle size, and they frequently contain impurities such as carbon and iron particles, giving a speckled appearance to the pale clay. Grog is made from ground-fired fireclay.

Three bowls by Fred Gatley, 1998. Polished bone china and porcelain with coloured inclusions, on patinated bronze bases with gold and silver additions. Photo Joel Degan.

Bone China

This is a difficult material to work with. It is a blend of china clay, feldspar and bone ash (or porcelain and bone ash), but, because of the high proportion of bone ash required, it lacks plasticity; for this reason it is most often used for casting, and is much used in industry. The potash in calcined animal bones acts as a bleaching agent, whitening the clay; this may also alter the colours of glazes used subsequently. A recipe might be 50/50 bone ash and porcelain, or 50 per cent bone ash/25 per cent china clay/25 per cent feldspar. Manufacturers are now including prepared bone-china bodies in their catalogues so it is becoming more accessible to studio potters; it is valued by them for its lightness and translucency.

Inclusions

Refractory materials and aggregates are added for various reasons, such as strength, whiteness or texture. They are usually coarser grained and of a larger particle size than the clay body. They may alter in firing but will not burn out, and therefore form an integral constituent of the fired clay.

Sand

Sand is mainly naturally ground quartz with a varying composition and grain size. Its main component is silica, but depending on its location it may also contain additives such as calcium from shells, soluble salts, or oxides which colour it and can give speckles in the fired clay. Sand gives a grainy texture to unfired clay, adding 'tooth' to a body which might otherwise feel too soft or slippery. It can act as a flux at high temperatures, altering the body by melting into glass.

Grog

Grog is made from clay, often fireclay, that has been fired, and ground down to varying particle sizes which are then graded by passing them through screens of different sized mesh. Grog is non-compressible with neutral shrinkage; like sand, it is used to open the body, to give texture and to reduce the risk of shrinkage and cracking in a

*R*elief by Roy Ashmore, 1998. Detail showing slate inclusions, surface partly broken away; fired to 1160°C.

clay body. It has been found that adding grogs of varying sizes to a body acts more effectively than using a uniform grade.

Shards

These are larger particles of ground-up fired clay or bricks, much coarser and more uneven than grog, and they are added to large or heavy pieces to give a particular textural effect. Some makers deliberately include disruptive elements in their clays to give a rough or broken texture, but care must be taken when handling them – slate, for instance, will splinter into sharp shards. They can be ball-milled to soften the edges, making working with them a little easier.

Aggregates

Some potters make their own aggregates specifically for each work. To do this, clay – frequently porcelain – is coloured with oxides or stains and fired to a low temperature, around 800°C to 900°C, then broken up and ground to the required size. At this temperature the ceramic is still quite soft and can be ground without difficulty, though if a large quantity is needed it may be best to do so using mechanical means. The resulting grits can be graded by passing them through sieves of decreasing mesh size. The clays chosen for aggregates should have a similar firing range to that being used for the body so as to avoid the risk of inclusions melting or erupting from the work, to equalize shrinkage as much as possible, and to encourage fusion. When the fired work is finished by sanding and polishing, the result will resemble granite or marble.

Surface detail from work by Felicity Aylieff, showing varied sizes of aggregates and glass inclusions.

Molochite

This substance is calcined china clay, usually finer than grog but graded in the same way, and used in whiteware for the same purposes. It is a relatively expensive material, and is most often used with porcelain.

Glass

Glass is usually introduced into a clay body as finely ground granules of varying sizes. Since it has been formed at very high temperatures it will not melt or alter in the firing unless this is very hot. It is usually introduced to create specks of colour and variety through a piece, and gives a particularly rich effect when the surface is ground and polished.

Organic Extras

Organic additions alter the handling characteristics of the raw clay but will burn out in the firing leaving only their imprint, with sometimes a trace of ash, in the texture of the body. Depending on the amount of organic material contained within it, the body may be rather porous, even after firing to high temperatures. This quality is sometimes exploited by makers in further smoke firings, since the carbon can be absorbed into the surface of the piece.

'Detail of a Torso' by Roy Ashmore. Straw and sawdust were added to the clay, and the piece made in a mould. After firing, the surface has been deliberately broken away to show the inner structure of the clay and the texture left by the additives when they burned out.

Fibres

Fibres of all sorts reduce plasticity, but help to bind the clay particles together in the raw state, thus also reducing the risk of cracking while working. Traditional potters all over the world have already learned by long experience to add suitable quantities of cow dung, rice straw or grasses – whatever is readily available – to their mix, along with juice from mesquite pods, liquid from the locust bean and other materials designed to harden the blocks, particularly when constructing large and semi-permanent structures such as houses built from adobe bricks or storage barns for grain. Nowadays some polymers or a proportion of cement may also be added as hardeners. Adobe bricks are unfired, but in a dry climate last for many years and are added to, or repaired with fresh clay as the need arises – just as paperclay may be added to, even when it is thoroughly dry.

Cellulose

This is the basis of all natural fibres: it is the product of photosynthesis, and the 'building block' from which fibres are formed. It is a straight-chain polymer of glucose (sugar), each unit linking to the next like a string of beads. Frequently, the longer the chain, the more stable the fibre – cotton, for example, has a long chain length and resists degradation and deterioration. Chemically, cellulose and glucose are carbohydrates consisting of carbon, hydrogen and oxygen, and cellulose is a ubiquitous constituent of the walls of every type of plant cell. Each cellulose fibre is thinner than a hair.

Cellulose comes in many forms, varying with the plant, but basically consists of sheets created from the glucose molecules which spiral round a hollow core called the lumen. Water can penetrate the lumen and be absorbed by the fibre. It is therefore described as hydrophilic, and can be large or small, with the cell walls thick or thin, depending on the plant type. The exterior of each tube consists of a substance known as lignin, its thickness again depending on the plant of origin. It is described as the cement that glues the fibres together, giving the plant the strength to grow straight and tall. Lignin is an amorphous polymer with no ordered structure. It is non-fibrous and is hydrophobic, repelling water. When degraded to form pulp, it leaves acidic residues that eventually turn paper yellow, and for that reason is not wanted in the papermaking process. Neither is it of much relevance to potters since it burns out in the fire. The traces of ash left by cellulose may act as a flux within the clay body.

Cellulose chains bond together, particularly when wet, and the important factor in making paperclay is the ability of its microscopic tubes to suck in clay and build a lattice-like structure. Cellulose may be included in paperclay in many guises: straw, grasses, cotton linters (the fine, shredded fibres used by papermakers), flax or shredded newsprint, which is normally made from woodpulp.

Plant fibres need treatment – usually boiling in an alkaline solution, then beating to break them down – before they are suitable for making into paper. In some plants, flax and hemp for example, the stem of the plant is used, while in others, such as cotton or kapok, the fibres are taken from around the seed pod. Some plant materials can cause an allergic reaction, and soda ash and lye used in papermaking are alkaline and corrosive on contact; chlorine, once used for bleaching, is also an irritant; however, it is now much less used. More recently a variety of shredded fibres is being prepared by

Standing tube drawing by Polly Macpherson, using pastel, hay and paint.

Standing tube structure by Polly Macpherson made from casting slip and hay, 1997. Sawdust smoked.

manufacturers specifically for use in paperclay and derived from these materials. These fibres are milled so fine that they can be added to some throwing bodies in small quantities, and a slip containing them can even be passed through a 60s mesh sieve. The addition of cellulose to a clay body gives paperclay a low shrinkage rate, and the ability of cellulose fibres to absorb several times their own weight of water without distorting the body is an important factor in its use.

Flax

This is the plant used for weaving linen, and its use as a clay additive is currently being assessed by at least one manufacturer. Studies have been carried out at the Keramisch Werkcentrum at Hertogenbosch in Holland which show that the fibres can be added directly to plastic clay without first being made into a pulp, and that only a very small percentage is necessary to strengthen the body without greatly altering its other characteristics.

Flax has a very long chain structure, and the original skeins of fibres consisting of a number of attached cells can be as long as 60cm (24in). This is important in weaving, and an advantage in papermaking, but would seem to be a disadvantage to potters unless very large pieces were being constructed. The Dutch experiments used flax fibres chopped to about 2.5cm (1in) long, and their conclusion was that their length had more importance than the plant source of the fibre, and that a mixture of long and short fibres was most satisfactory, requiring less fibre to be added.

Flax also contains oils, some of which remain in the treated fibres, and research is continuing into whether this will be an advantage in improving frost resistance for pieces which are to be sited outdoors and subjected to freezing and thawing.

Sawdust

This is mostly used in bricks or for large sculptural pieces. It burns away leaving large air pockets which open the body greatly, making it very porous as well as allowing heat to pass through. Woodpulp is a main ingredient of newsprint, though in a much finer form, and has a shorter fibre length, particularly if it has been recycled. This may be why some makers find it rather soft and sloppy in use, not adding much to the character of the finished paperclay body.

Fibreglass

Made from silica first spun into fine glass threads, then woven to form a textile, the tissue version being even thinner than tissue paper. The threads of fibreglass are not hollow and so the material is not absorbent, the clay slip being held by the mesh of the weave. At high temperatures – over 1200°C – the fibreglass melts and the silica fuses within the body, so at that point the proportion of silica already present in the clay is crucial: if it is too high it will cause so much fluxing that the body itself begins to melt and slump. The fibreglass material has become an ingredient.

Nylon

Chopped finely and added to clay in quite a small proportion (about 1–2 per cent, or a handful to a 23-litre (5-gallon) bucket of sloppy clay), nylon fibres improve its green strength and handling qualities in the raw state; however, the fibres are not hollow and can only absorb a small amount of the water from the clay slip. The material has a certain elasticity which is felt by some to make clay containing it less suitable for throwing, but it acts as a useful reinforcement in handbuilding bodies. Nylon melts and burns out at a relatively low temperature (260°C); furthermore it smoulders rather than flares, and the fumes are less noxious than those of polyester.

Bowl form with fluted rim by Frederick Payne. Fibreglass tissue dipped in porcelain slip; layered and embossed. Photo Alan Bye.

Polyester

This material has a similar melting point, but flares as it burns, giving off fumes which are unpleasant, and which must be vented away. It is chopped into short lengths and is used for the same reasons (and in the same proportions) as nylon, behaving in a similar manner when used for handbuilding. Some of those who use it feel that it has less elasticity than nylon, and is active and more stable in a mix. This, combined with the fact that it does not absorb any water, means that a clay containing it can be suitable for throwing, though the difference would only be noticed if the work was thrown quite thinly.

'Basset Hound' by Brendan Hesmondhalgh. Raku/craft crank clay mix with polyester fibres; fired to 1260°C. 86cm (38in) long × 29cm (11in) high. Photo Andrew Sanderson.

Vermiculite/Mica

An alumina silicate mineral made from Montmorillonite; in granular form it is often used in compost to assist drainage, and in building materials as an insulation. It absorbs water up to a temperature of 550°C, and is used by potters in large-scale work to give lightness. It burns away in the firing leaving gaps within the clay body.

Perlite

Perlite is another silica-based additive, also used in the building industry for its thermal properties. It consists of mica particles which have been heated to expand like popcorn. On firing, the granules revert to their original size leaving cavities containing only a tiny bit of mica. Perlite absorbs water and shrinks on firing, leaving a deposit of mica and becoming brittle. For this reason it is better used in bodies which are to be fired only at lower temperatures, such as raku.

Many makers use combinations of more than one additive, seeking different qualities from several so that each may combine to provide a material best suited to the specific needs of the work in hand.

4 Making Paperclay

However you go about it, making clay – paper or otherwise – is a messy business, so it is as well to make as much as you are likely to need for a cycle of work all at once in a single mix. Unless measurements are very accurate and materials very consistent there are likely to be slight variations in each batch, and while paperclay is very tolerant in combining with other materials in a way that would not be possible with conventional clays, it could be annoying to run out just before finishing a piece and to have to complete with a slightly different blend.

The idea is simple. An amount of paper pulp (most sorts of paper) is combined with an equal or larger amount of clay (any sort of clay), frequently in the form of slip; the whole is well mixed and then dried out to a workable consistency, and it can then be used in an infinite variety of ways. The finished and fired material will resemble the original clay, the fibres from the paper having burned out to leave the original clay matrix. Therefore the type of clay used should be suitable for the eventual finished piece. However, because of the greatly increased green strength given by the presence of the fibres, much more complex structures can be created than would be possible with the clay on its own. Porcelain, for instance, can be used for sculptures on a scale that would not normally be feasible.

The danger is that the material is so easy to use that unstable pieces may be made, which either slump in the kiln or collapse when out of it. A weak piece will always be weak, and though the strength of paperclay will disguise this initially, the fire will ruthlessly expose flaws and design faults.

> **Tip**
>
> The addition of fireclay grog to local clays whose composition may be variable will lengthen the firing range and make the clay less likely to slump suddenly in the kiln.

Making Slip

Slip is basically clay mixed with water to the consistency of thickish cream. It should pour without being too sluggish or lumpy, so that a stick drawn around the surface will make a swirl mark but will not remain upright for more than a few moments if left in the bucket. Finer particles will obviously blend more easily than coarse, heavy bodies; sand or grog tends to sink to the bottom of the bucket in a heavy sediment and will need frequent stirring, and therefore clays with a reasonable ballclay content will make a smoother, and possibly more satisfactory slip. Prepared clays already contain all the

necessary ingredients, and many potters use scraps and turnings from their normal clay to make their paperclay slip. This is fine if only a small amount is needed; however, it will not be sufficient for large-scale work.

Casting slip contains deflocculent which reduces the amount of water in the mix and therefore cuts down on the drying-out process later on, and potters who already cast their work find this type of slip a convenient material to use.

Mixing Slip

Plastic clay seems to take more mixing to break down smoothly, possibly because the particles are already saturated and cannot easily absorb more water. Some makers slice off clay from the bag, or from several bags if they are blending clays, then add it to the water in handfuls either torn into small lumps or squeezed through the fingers. The resulting slip can be screened through a 60s or 80s mesh sieve if it is felt necessary to even out the consistency; however, anything much

*M*ixing *clays: an efficient, trouble-free mixer, capable of dealing with moderate quantities, and easily lifted from one bucket to another. From left to right the buckets contain: newspaper pulp well soaked, with surplus water drained off but still sloppy; stoneware clay made into a thick slip before pulp is added; sieved porcelain slip; the same porcelain slip with pulp added. The grey colour comes from the newsprint and burns out in the firing, leaving the clay white.*

Tip
In general, mixing dry is not a good idea because of the dust factor – weighed ingredients should always be added to a measured amount of water one by one and allowed to disperse into the liquid with gentle stirring before the next material is added, rather than pouring water onto a bucket full of dry, powdery materials. Once a certain amount of water has been absorbed, the whole can be thoroughly blended with a power mixer, but if this is used too soon the dust will really fly. Even better is to perform the whole operation in a closed blunger.

finer might screen out too many of the 'opener' particles and could weaken the body. For a coarse sculptural body it may not be necessary to sieve at all, while for a porcelain that is to be rolled very thin and smooth a finer mesh – 100, or even 120 – may be better.

Tools for the Job

Mixer

Small quantities can be mixed using an electric drill with a paint-mixer blade attachment, and some use a food blender; but while this is useful for tests, it is very labour intensive when used for any volume. A heavy duty mixer is a wise investment which will very quickly pay for itself in terms of time and energy saved in mixing clays, slips and glazes; it will last for years, needing no maintenance apart from cleaning.

Blunger

Likewise, a blunger is invaluable for mixing larger amounts of slip, usually 68 or 90 litres (15 or 20 gallons) at a time. Once a satisfactory recipe has been formulated, it is simple to make slip from dry materials, and the mix will last for months if needs be, always remaining consistent. The drawback is that changes cannot easily be made to the recipe or a new version made up until the blunger is emptied. Once a satisfactory formula has been arrived at, however, it is a great help to have additional quantities of slip always available, either to add as surface layers for a smoother effect than the slightly rough texture of paperclay, or to add colour when blended with additional oxides and stains.

A blunger can also be used for breaking down paper into pulp: put the water in first, and then add the torn paper gradually. This can take some time, but the machine can go on mixing while you do other things. Every so often clumps of paper gather on the blades and these will have to be cleared off, so this assumes a machine with sufficient aperture to allow you to reach inside.

Doughmixer

This is normally used for making plastic clay on a large scale, and is a big investment in terms of both cost and space; however, it would be invaluable where several potters share a workshop, or where large sculptures are being made. It is an easy job to add the right proportion of paper pulp to the rest of the materials in the mixer, and a large quantity of paperclay may be mixed with no more effort than when making a normal clay batch. This is the method used by Lotte Glob, a Danish potter living in the north of Scotland who adds in whatever selection of materials the work being made seems to demand. The proportions vary till the mix feels right.

A few years ago it was possible to acquire doughmixers from bakeries quite cheaply, as small local businesses closed down, or health and safety regulations in the food industry required different standards; however, that no longer seems to be the case. Nevertheless, doughmixers have a very long life so they can still be found, sometimes through firms refurbishing secondhand pottery machinery, or at auction sales. Most types need a three-phase electricity supply.

Choosing the Paper

Paper is described by Frank Hamer as being composed of vegetable cellulose fibres which are:

> … strong and resilient, expanding and contracting reversibly with the intake or evaporation of water. This is why paper pulp is such an ideal opener for a clay body, and why wet can be added to dry.

As an additive, paper has the advantage of being readily available in many different forms, as well as being cheap, or very often free. Potters have tried all sorts – egg and apple boxes, newsprint, shredded computer paper, toilet tissue – and the only types which seem to be universally disliked (because they take so long to break down) are the shiny coated papers used in quality magazines for colour photography. Ironically these papers are the ones containing the highest proportion of china clay in their composition. Cardboard is also difficult because it contains glues which make it hard to break down, and unsatisfactory in use.

Spruce. Woodcut by William Geissler, reproduced by permission from Tullis Russell, papermakers.

Tip
Newspaper usually tears easily on the length. If you try tearing a newspaper you will find that it tears straight in one direction, but is not easily torn neatly in the other.

A good test of a paper's suitability is the ease with which it can be torn. Papers with short fibres tear most easily and are most easily broken down, though papermakers look for the greater strength given by longer fibres for their handmade papers. Papers containing rags are good because of the high proportion of cotton or linen contained in them, as are the papers used by artists – but these are generally too expensive to be torn up, unless the drawings on them are embarassingly bad! Newsprint is largely made from woodpulp which has shorter fibres, and there is a theory that the fibres in recycled paper are also shorter, though so

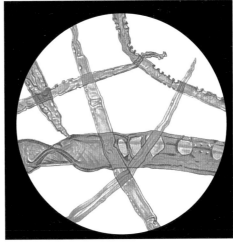

*D*rawing of wood fibre by William Geissler (above), *enlarged 300 times. The woodpulp from both trees is extensively used for many types of paper.*

*P*ine. *Woodcut by William Geissler, as opposite.*

many recycled papers are made now from varying mixes that an exact formula is hard to ascertain.

Varieties of Paper

Different papers behave in different ways in the raw state, but differences after firing are not so easy to detect. For instance, newsprint gives a dirty-looking grey sludge which can make the paperclay look grimy, but this is caused by the printing inks and will burn out, leaving the work the colour of the original clay body. Newsprint also gives the paperclay a slightly soft and floppy feeling (due to the shorter fibres in the wood pulp), which is good for modelling, or where the paperclay will be wedged to make a solid mass rather than left in thinner sheets.

Egg boxes have a strong, firm feeling when the paperclay is in the raw state, and are good for larger sheets and for making constructions because the sheets are easy to handle; but after firing there is no ascertainable difference except perhaps for a slightly rougher surface texture if the clay has not been rolled. Toilet tissue is the fibre favoured by many makers, perhaps because it is easy to obtain, clean, soft and quick to mix, and looks pretty, particularly when coloured – but it has no measurable advantages over other pulp, and it seems a pity to have to buy a new product just to break it up!

Tip
Toilet tissue can be pressure-cooked for about ten minutes to make it easy to break down into pulp. Paper will break down to pulp more quickly if hot water is used.

*C*otton. Woodcut by William Geissler, as before. The fibres from the seed of the plant, known as linters, are used for papermaking (right).

*T*he fibres from cotton, enlarged 300 times. From a drawing by William Geissler (far right).

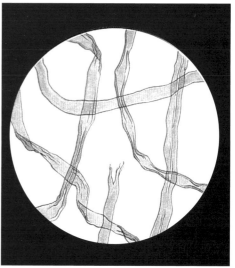

*R*eady-made fibres available from the manufacturers. Those shown are (top left) shredded cotton, finely milled newsprint (bottom left), very finely milled cellulose (bottom right), and much coarser shredded denim (top right). Photo Claire Brown.

Shredded computer or photocopier paper is the most satisfactory to use from all points of view, in the opinion of many potters. The original paper is of good quality, it is already in narrow strips and easy to break up, it is ubiquitous, would otherwise be waste, is clean to use – and it is free! It also makes good paperclay.

Ready-Made Fibres

One or two manufacturers in Britain are now selling cellulose-based materials such as finely shredded cotton and denim as well as papers as suitable additions for making paperclay. These save all the effort of tearing and soaking the original pulp, and arrive fluffy and clean, just needing to be wetted before being added to the mix. They have passed health and safety standards if used in the prescribed way. Some are so fine that they can even be screened through a 60s mesh sieve. A selection of these has been tested, and the results are analysed in Chapter 6.

Economic Logic?

In America and Australia clay containing fibre is already on sale at the same price as ordinary clays, which makes its increasing use even more likely. The advantages of using fibreclay for certain types of work are not in question. However, in a survey sent out to colleges and individuals in Britain, many potters who replied to the question of why they used paperclay stated that they wanted to use materials such as waste paper which would otherwise be discarded and end up in landfill sites, and that this was an important factor in their choice. They were also very concerned about costs, wanting to make use of cheaper materials whenever this did not compromise the quality of the work being made. Both of these responses might seem to argue towards making your own material rather than buying ready made, but potters are notoriously bad at costing their work so it might be a salutary exercise to tot up all the preparation time, adding that to the time spent actually making, then balance the whole against the cost of purchasing prepared materials. Perhaps it is just a question of time before the latter take over.

Making the Pulp

Again the method is simple – but very, very boring. Paper is torn up and mixed with water till the segments have disintegrated into a porridge-like sludge in which no separate pieces can be seen. This is then combined with the clay in varying proportions.

Making the pulp takes longer and uses more water than you could possibly anticipate. It helps if the water is hot, or at least fairly warm, as this seems to break up the paper more quickly. Add the torn up or shredded paper in handfuls to half a bucket of water, mixing well all the time to prevent the paper clinging together in impenetrable clumps which will prove hard to break up later. Continue mixing till the pieces can no longer be seen separately, and check that none are piling up at the bottom of the bucket. Sometimes it seems easier to do a preliminary mix, then leave it all to soak overnight, finishing the process the following day. As the paper breaks down into pulp it soaks up an incredible amount of water, so more may need to be added during mixing. It is better to use a lot of water at this stage as it will make a more even mix, and any surplus can simply be drained off later. It may help to weigh the contents of whatever beaker or container is being used both for slip and pulp, and to note the weights of the most satisfactory mix in order to maintain future consistency.

Combining the Mix

Having made the clay slip and the paper pulp, the two need to be blended in a ratio that is suitable both for the type of clay used and for the work to be made. There are wide variations in the way potters calculate this, but most measure in volume rather than by weight, the proportion varying from a very small addition of about 5 per cent wet paper pulp to as much as 50 per cent. Most find a volume between 20 and 30 per cent to be the most satisfactory amount.

Some potters prefer to squeeze out the excess water from the paper pulp before adding it to the slip. This is easily done by putting it in a cloth or a porous bag and hanging it like a hammock so that the water can drain out; this can then be squeezed a bit more by hand so that the pulp is damp, but no longer dripping. Tiny test amounts can be drained through a sieve.

Other potters just pick up handfuls and squeeze. This method means that less water will be added to the clay mix, although it may make it harder to calculate with any degree of accuracy the amount of pulp being added. Luckily exact measurements are not crucial: 'About a cricket ball to two litres' was one description given. A ruler or marked stick standing inside a bucket containing a known quantity of slip will show the increase in volume, and will act as an aid to measurement.

Other potters do not make the clay into slip, but merely add handfuls of plastic clay (squeezed through the fingers to break it up into smaller pieces) to the bucket of sloppy pulp until the consistency feels right. Another group adds powdered clay to the sloppy paper pulp until the mixture feels stiff enough. Both these methods need thorough beating to ensure the mix is sufficiently well blended.

A Really Easy Way

My preferred system is to let both clay slip and pulp stand in their separate buckets for at least twenty-four hours, or even longer so that they can settle, then pour off all the surplus water from the surface of both buckets before mixing. The contents of both should have a similar consistency, and it is then simple to mix two (or three) jugfuls of slip with one of pulp, and because both are liquid they blend quickly and evenly. The mix is very wet, but another twenty-four hours or so and the surplus water will again have risen to the top and can be poured off without difficulty.

*M*aking paperclay sheets. The paperclay slip is poured onto a plaster slab with wooden framing around the edge to contain it. Fillets of wood of varying depth can be used to make sheets of different thicknesses. A strip across the frame levels the surface (left).

*A*fter a few moments the clay slip has stiffened sufficiently for the frame to be pulled away, leaving a torn edge which many makers like and make use of. In an hour or two the clay will be firm enough to be peeled from the plaster (above).

Planning

It is always a good idea, provided there is the space, to be preparing materials in an ongoing sequence so that work is not held up by lack of the right clay or slip at the precise moment it is required. Nothing is more destructive of a creative roll than finding that you are unable to get on to the next stage because the particular materials needed are not ready, and by the time a new batch is made the original idea may have flown and be hard to recapture. The ability to work at speed with paperclay is an exciting factor for many who use it, and is also one reason why some prefer to raw glaze, or not glaze at all. The whole process becomes more direct and immediate, and the original ideas for finishing are not forgotten in the bisque firing.

Time is a precious commodity, and one that most creative people find they never have enough of. Ideas may take time to mature and have a long gestation period at the back of the mind, but once they are out in the open the working-out stage wants to be untrammelled by problems of materials or techniques.

Making Life Easier

Plaster batts, cast to fit an old baker's trolley and positioned near a kiln, are an easy way to dry paperclay and stack a large amount in a small space.

Natural processes can help the potter, given enough time. For instance:

- Slices of plastic clay will dry out on their own to a state where they can quite easily be crumbled or broken down to add to water to make a slip.
- If lumps of clay are left to soak in water over a period of time they will dissolve, gradually becoming a slip on their own, so to speak, and requiring very little beating.
- Papers, too, if left to soak, will absorb water, swell and soften, and start to break up.
- Heavy sand or grit will sink to the bottom of a bucket so the finer particles can be decanted from the top for slip, and clay will settle so that excess water can be poured off.

This can all be happening quietly and continuously under the bench, and it takes only a moment or two each day to decant liquid, stir a mix, or blend clay and pulp together ready to dry out when needed.

Drying Out

The type of work to be made will determine the way in which the slurry is dried out. The

Tip
Carefully lifting one corner of the board once or twice after the mould is full and tapping it down on the bench will encourage any air bubbles to rise to the surface, and will also help level off the surface of the plaster when casting batts.

paperclay needs to be poured or scooped onto a dry, porous surface, its thickness decided by the needs of the finished work. Porcelain sheets for printing can be poured very thin, only needing a little rolling to smooth and compress the surface later on. The correct thickness for tiles or slabs can be gauged by using wooden strips and levelling off, or chunkier amounts can be made with a frame around a plaster slab, the clay being turned over after some time so that it dries evenly.

Plaster Batts

Many potters do not like having plaster in the studio, but treated with care, it is a very suitable material to use for making drying batts. It is very absorbent and, depending on the water content of the clay mix and the warmth of the atmosphere, several sheets can usually be made on one slab in a day. A board covered with stretched canvas or hessian makes a good alternative, and a thick wodge of paper can be inserted between board and cloth for added absorbency if this is needed.

An old baker's trolley with shelves made to fit the runners makes an efficient drying rack, taking up very little space and allowing a large number of sheets of paperclay to be made and dried out easily. If the rack is positioned near the kiln or an alternative source of heat, the clay will dry quickly and the water will evaporate from the batts, enabling them to be used again with little delay. Air circulation is as effective in drying as heat, and may be even better since the clay will dry more evenly, so a strategically placed fan or old vacuum cleaner – set to blow, rather than suck – can work well, providing it does not also blow clouds of dust through the workshop.

Lotte Glob dries her paperclay on kiln shelves covered with a layer of newspaper, and spreads it on 'like butter'; and in her book, Rosette Gault mentions making very large slabs for sculpture on the floor – but the concrete wasn't very absorbent and they took ten days to dry to a liftable state! In Norway, Janet Casson dries sheets for her lifesize figures on thick piles of newspaper on the floor, then rolls them up before they become leather hard, keeping them wrapped in plastic. Lorraine Fernie uses canvas over a thick board; and Peter Hicks spreads his slurry onto builders' plasterboard.

Storage

As soon as the clay is firm enough it can be peeled from the batt and either used or stored. My own method is to lay each slab on a separate piece of old cotton sheeting and pile several one on top of the other, then to wrap the whole bundle in plastic until needed. The sheeting means that the clay slabs can be lifted easily, without distortion, and they do not stick together. Leaving the clay on newspaper at this stage is not a good idea as the paper very soon becomes saturated and tears, leaving irritating shreds which must be peeled from the paperclay sheet before it can be used. If the clay is to be rolled out more thinly later on it can stay on the same cloth, and the cloth can also be used to carry the clay in the workshop if it is to be sprayed with coloured slips or put through any other processes before being assembled. However, it also means that every so often a heap of grotty cloths will have to be washed, making the workshop look more like Widow Twankey's laundry than a studio; and in the meantime care must be taken to avoid contaminating new clay with stains or slips from used cloths. With a bit of experience it should be possible to calculate the likely amount of paperclay needed for a particular series of work, and to make just enough to last without having to store it damp for too long.

Ideally paperclay should be used soon after it is made; if this is not possible, the clay sheets can be allowed to dry out until they are needed, when – such is the amazing nature of this clay – they can be damped again and used as normal. Some slight plasticity may be lost, but the ability of paperclay to soak up water through the hollow tubes of the cellulose without the whole structure becoming soggy allows dry clay to be joined to dry, or dry to be combined with wet, with no difficulty and no problems of cracking. Brian Gartside lives in New Zealand: he dries his slabs on plaster until they are hard, then stores the bone-dry clay sheets on edge until they are needed; like this he finds they do not warp. Slabs that are to be bent or curved can then be immersed in a bath of water for about three hours; for straight, flat-sided pieces only the edges need to be damped and they can then be joined as usual. He also suggests storing wet paperclay in sealed plastic bags in the deep freeze if it is to be kept for any length of time – though this is something yet to be checked. In England, John Dowling makes his paperclay in bulk by pouring the slurry into wooden frames on top of cloth-covered thick plaster slabs; he then cuts it into ingot-like blocks when it is dry enough to handle. The blocks are allowed to dry out completely, and are stored till needed. To make them workable again they are soaked in a tray of water for several hours or overnight.

The above method can also be applied to used scraps. Dried pieces can be kept and easily soaked down for re-use when needed, and many potters also keep a bucket of wet slurry for use in joining edges or for coating onto the surface of the constructed work to alter the texture. Small quantities can best be stored in tightly lidded containers.

There is very little waste with paperclay because of the ease with which it can be recycled, or damped and re-used – another factor in its favour.

M*ould has developed on a sheet of paperclay stored damp for several months. The clay was on a cloth wrapped in plastic, and still quite damp and pliable. Exposure to sunlight will kill off spores, and the mould does not harm the fired clay, but it does smell, and anyone susceptible to chest ailments should wear a mask and add bleach or vinegar to the clay mix. Alternatively it may be stored dry, and re-wetted as needed.*

Moulds and Spores

As already mentioned, most conventional clays will improve with age, becoming more plastic and good to use so long as they are not allowed to dry out; however, this is not the case with paperclays. The organic material rots and disintegrates, and black mould spores can form on the surface of the clay, producing a very unpleasant smell. Many potters have overcome such problems by adding ½ to one teaspoonful of bleach per bucket of clay to prevent, or at least delay, the formation of mould. The sterilizing fluid used for babies' bottles has been suggested as a gentler alternative to bleach, as has vinegar. My own buckets have been left standing for weeks at a time; they have a film of water on the surface, and this seems to act as a seal because there is no smell until the water is poured off and the mixture stirred. Standing the clay in the sun gets rid of moulds: it is in a damp, humid atmosphere that they flourish.

Tip
Half a spoonful of Milton, the substance used to sterilize babies' bottles, has been suggested as being more user-friendly than bleach. Others use vinegar in small quantities.

Safety

Cellulose is organic and can produce allergic reactions. It is not a problem I have encountered to any extent, but John Lawrence in New Zealand became so ill with respiratory problems that he needed treatment with antibiotics. Perhaps the colder, less humid temperatures in this country and the freezing workshops of many British potters make a difference; however, it is not a problem to be lightly dismissed.

Those with allergies or any sort of chest ailment should take care not to breathe in spores by wearing a mask while working with paperclay. It may help to wear thin surgical gloves for some processes. A large amount of paper is now recycled and may have undergone numerous treatments in the process. There is much more concern for the environment than there used to be, and papers are bleached with oxygen rather than the chlorine previously used – but paper may still contain substances which provoke sensitive reactions in some people.

It is always important to keep the atmosphere as dust free as possible. This is easier with paperclay since the fibres bond the clay together and the material is less likely to be used for sanded surfaces or for carving. Working with damp materials is less likely to create dust, and if scraping or rubbing down is necessary it should be done over a basin of water so that the particles fall downwards and are absorbed into the water, rather than left in a heap on the bench where they can be scattered and breathed in.

It is better to mop the floor than to brush it, and work surfaces should be wiped down regularly so as not to contaminate work in progress with unwanted foreign bodies from previous creations.

Tip
Clay should *never* be sanded dry whether it is fired or raw. *Always* use wet and dry paper or diamond-coated abrasives which are water fed. When scraping down or carving, have the work near the edge of the bench and a bowl of water below so that scrapings can fall or be brushed into the water and do not blow round the studio.

5 Recipes

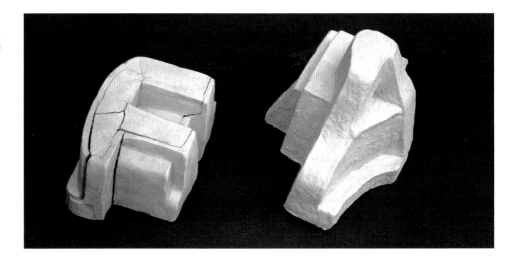

In the early research for this book a questionnaire was sent out to colleges and, through requests for information in ceramic magazines, to all those known to be using paper-clay or clay with significant additions. Many makers had come independently to very similar conclusions regarding proportions and suitable materials. For paper pulp, shredded computer paper and toilet tissue were most favoured, often because they were readily available, either free or cheap, and could be broken down easily, rather than for any particular qualities they gave to the fired clay.

Newspaper was less popular, possibly since it takes longer to tear up and dissolve, and the print makes the resulting pulp an unpleasant dirty grey colour – though this burns away without leaving any trace. Newsprint contains a high percentage of wood pulp (that has a high proportion of lignin, the reason for it being harder to break down) as well as recycled papers, so that its composition is variable and harder to determine. Some makers also felt it did not give sufficient character to the finished body.

Many had started using paperclay from curiosity to see what it could do that other clays could not; and many spoke of the ecological implications of recycling a waste material which would otherwise go into landfill sites. Cost was also mentioned, and although the time in preparation must be counted in this equation, the economy of using less clay and firing it to lower temperatures is another relevant factor. Many found that they could use cheaper clays – the clay from local brickworks was often chosen for sculptural work – and that it was easy to make a slip from recycled clay scraps;

but porcelain, an expensive choice, was also much used, favoured mostly for its whiteness and fineness when printing.

The qualities most enjoyed by the material created were its ambiguity, and the hybrid quality that allowed it to behave like paper or card for printing, to be thick or thin, to be draped or wrapped like a textile, and to be cast in large sheets without the effort of rolling big slabs. An added attraction appeared to be the low-tech aspect of paperclay: very few tools or special equipment are needed, and slab rollers, wheel or damp cupboard are redundant; some makers even manage without a kiln, taking minimalism even further. Other advantages mentioned included:

- Wedging is no longer a big chore. Scraps can be soaked in a bucket for use as joining slip, or dried out for re-use. Larger components or sections not used can be kept in a dry state and used, even months later, in other work.
- Breaks no longer mean the end of a piece. Slip or patches can be used for repairs, and even fired work can have raw clay joins.
- Work which does not feel right can easily be cut apart to be reworked or have new pieces added.
- Large work can be fired in sections to fit in the kiln and joined afterwards.

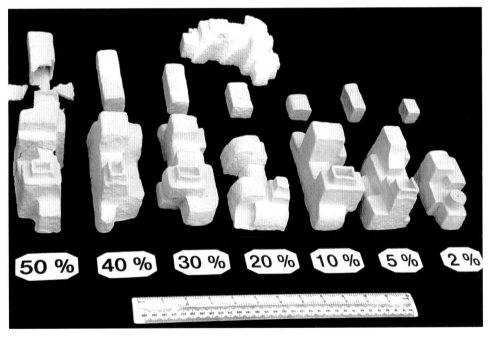

*T*est pieces by Frank Smith using various percentages of paper. The pieces were completely enclosed, and built over a complex armature of expanded polystyrene, such as can be seen at the back of the photo. None of the pieces cracked in the firing (the damage to the 50 per cent piece was caused by handling), demonstrating that the material remains porous, allowing gases and moisture to escape.

Recipes for Paperclay Bodies

The proportions of clay to pulp varied from 50/50 at the highest ratio to 80/20 at the lower end of the scale, the type of clay not making much difference to the amounts of pulp added; most settled for about two parts of clay to one of pulp, measured by volume rather than by weight.

This section gives some recipes for paperclay bodies that have been developed by different makers for specific purposes, and that have been found to work for certain effects. They are all the result of curiosity and experimentation, and are meant to be a guide for further exploration rather than exact scientific measurements to be slavishly followed. In many cases exact measurements have not been found necessary – 'a handful in a bucket' could be open to a wide variety of interpretations – and a knowledge of the materials being used, based on previous experience, has been found sufficient.

Two vessel forms by Carol Farrow, 1998. These are made from slabs of Earthstone clay and pulp, incised and pressed onto fabric before assembling, then fired to 1280°C. They are then coloured with oxides and refired to 1100°C.

CAROL FARROW was one of the early developers of paperclay because she found porcelain was not sufficiently robust for the large pieces she wanted to make; she therefore used T-material or 'White St Thomas' instead, and more recently she has also been using 'White Earthstone'. Proportions vary from 50/50 to 70/30 clay to pulp. Carol is also a papermaker, and prefers to use cotton seed linters for the fibre content, sometimes mixed with some computer paper. Papermakers want long fibres to give strength to the paper, but length is of less importance to potters, and in fact makes cutting or modelling more difficult. Carol casts large, thin sheets for constructions, as well as thick, solid pieces in a mould, when the plaster absorbs excess water and other objects can be embedded in the clay body. The solid pieces are often finished by smoke firing.

JANET CASSON makes lifesize figures and animal forms for which she requires a strong body. She currently uses Vingerling white grogged stoneware, though she has also worked with crank and a school buff body, using 10kg (22lb) soft plastic clay to 1kg (2.2lb) soaked pulp from shredded office paper. This is mixed up in batches of 30–40kg (66–88lb) at a time with a hand mixer.

ROSALIND SIMPSON uses white earthenware to make a slip, to which she adds 28 per cent paper pulp. This is fired to 1000°C for the bisque temperature, and 1140°C for the glaze.

JANET HAMER uses powdered porcelain with toilet tissue in a ratio of three parts clay to one of pulp for her lustred bird forms. This is 'slop cast' – to use her description – by pouring it into a plaster mould and pulling it up the sides to reach the desired thickness.

JAL FRAMJI studied at Wolverhampton, a college where individual experimentation is encouraged, and from where much information has come. He is interested in geological formations, wanting a heavily textured body to which he can add oxides and

Composite of several clays including porcelain by Jal Framji (recipes in text). Fired to 1250°C, sandblasted and waxed.

Clay composite by Jal Framji (as previous picture). One clay is bubbling and melting.

stains, and sandblasting after firing to reveal inner areas. Here are the results of some of his tests:

Coloured Body
H.T.G.	81%	(a cheap brown stoneware clay)
Spodumene	9%	
Ilmenite	2%	
Rutile	2%	
Red stain	6%	

With this body, spodumene affects the clay, making it more reactive as quantity is increased. (Spodumene is lithium feldspar, and contains alumina and silica as well as lithium. It tends to have a lower expansion rate than most feldspars and is sometimes used in flameproof bodies.) Small quantities of lithium can also be added, as well as petalite.

Brick Body
Brick clay	75%
Lead bisilicate	15%
Manganese dioxide	2%
Various stains	8%

This body uses a coarse local brick clay. By overfiring it and adding manganese it melts and becomes frothy, though this can be controlled by temperature and the amount of manganese added. Vermiculite and sawdust may also be added for greater strength. This body is used for its effect when layered with other clays.

Light Clay
Ash White   71.2%
(white stoneware clay)
China clay   17.8%
Rutile   4%
Yellow stain   6%
Vanadium pentoxide   1%

All these bodies contain elements that are reactive, and will bubble or melt at different temperatures. Pieces are fired twice, the second time in a container, reaching 1250°C. The materials are first mixed dry, then pulp is added to make paperclay and, when sufficiently blended and stiffened, the different clays are wedged loosely together, not mixing them too much; other combustible materials such as straw or cloth are sometimes also added at this stage.

Detail of stacked form by Liz Cave. Fired to 1260°C. Cut into with diamond saw.

LIZ CAVE uses the same clays to make casting slips. To 10kg (22lb) of clay (craft crank, HTG or Ash White) she adds 10g (0.35oz) of soda ash and 10g of sodium silicate, and uses the resulting slips to layer in moulds, adding sawdust of varying degrees of coarseness in percentages up to 50 per cent; 10 per cent bright blue stain is added to some for colouring. She has also tried other amazing combustibles, amongst them teabags, cotton wool and cat litter, although she doesn't describe exactly what characteristics they left behind.

BELINDA SWINGLER works in Belgium, and is another who tries audacious mixtures. She lists nut shells, mint, onion skins, tobacco plant, seeds and leaves among more usual additions such as sawdust and varied sorts of papers (including the telephone directory) as additives to a selection of clays. The vegetable matter was not a success, being difficult to work with and giving a lumpy surface, and – as might have been expected – the nut shells left large holes in the structure. Her usual mixture is 70 per cent dry clay to 30 per cent pulp, with the addition of up to 10 per cent bentonite.

URSULA KUPFER in Switzerland had been working for some time with coloured clays, but found that the different shrinkage rates of the clays caused problems; paperclay solved these difficulties. She uses office paper, torn and soaked in hot water overnight, then one part of the resulting pulp is mixed with five parts naturally coloured local clay (called Odenwalder, Niederahrer and Manganton). Smaller, rolled pieces may be fired within saggers containing steel wool, cow dung, pine needles, seaweed, copper wire or salt. For sculptural work, only about one part of pulp will be added to ten parts of clay, possibly with a small addition of fine grog or sand.

'*The Countryside Walks – Easter?' by Belinda Swingler, 1999. This piece contains many of the events of a cross-country walk. 31 × 35cm (12 × 14in). Fired to 1260°C.*

Rolls by Ursula Kupfer, made from porcelain paperclay. Sawdust fired, with copper and iron sulphate sprinkled in to give colour. 30–60cm (12–24in).

PAUL BRADLEY uses a blunger to make quite large quantities of a semi-porcelain casting slip. Here is the recipe he gives, in the order that the ingredients are added to the blunger:

17 litres (3gal 5pt) water plus 0.075kg (2½oz) Dispex*
15kg (33lb) BCC Grolleg china clay
7.5kg (16.5lb) Hyplas 64 ballclay
7.5kg (16.5lb) Quartz 200 mesh
2.5kg (5.5lb) FFF Potash Feldspar

* Dispex is the name of a proprietary deflocculent.

Paul writes:

> Time should always be allowed for the materials to be absorbed into the water in the blunger (or a bucket). Add ingredients one at a time, clays first and heavier materials after, with gaps between each addition to give time for thorough mixing.

John Lawrence building a vessel form. John also makes and grinds his own coloured grogs.

JOHN LAWRENCE in New Zealand makes his clay body from this recipe:

Grolleg china clay	200
White ballclay	260
Nepheline syenite	240
Flint	200
Molochite /grog	100

To this is added toilet roll pulp for paperclay. John makes his pulp by soaking a toilet roll in neat bleach overnight, then squeezing it out wearing rubber gloves before blunging it in hot water using an electric paint mixer. This is added to the dry clay, about half a roll to the clay quantities listed.

He makes his oxides and stains into fine grogs by mixing them with an engobe slip, calcining to 995°C, then grinding them finely in a simple homemade grinder.

Slip Recipe

China clay	20%
White ballclay	20%
Nepheline syenite	25%
Flint	30%
Alkaline frit	5%

ANGELA MELLOR in Australia was at first unable to find a suitable bone china casting slip, so she devised her own; however, one manufacturer is now producing one which she also uses. This is the recipe for her own bone china casting slip:

Eckalite No. 1 kaolin	30%
Bone ash – natural	45%
Potash feldspar	22.8%
Silica	2.2%
To this is added	2g Dispex per dry kilo weight
	1g sodium silicate
	600ml water per dry kilo wt of material

Water-soluble colourants (mainly nitrates and chlorides) are applied in strengths between 1 per cent and 10 per cent, though if they are too strong the translucency is lost.

'Glacial Light': a group of bone china bowls from a series by Angela Mellor, 1999. Inlaid with paperclay at top rim. The largest is 17cm (7in) diameter × 13cm (5in) high; the middle one is 10cm (4in) diameter × 8cm (3in) high; and the smallest 10cm (4in) diameter × 8cm (3in) high. Fired to 1250°C; oxidized.

CAROL RAY NINO works in Spain and makes a porcelain paperclay which she fires to a very hot 1300°C. For this she adds 100g (3.53oz) molochite and 30g (1oz) bentonite to 500g (1.1lb) pulp made from toilet tissue, before adding in 1kg (2.2lb) plastic porcelain clay and mixing by hand. She uses this for work as diverse in scale from buttons and beads to mural panels.

Paperclay porcelain teapot by Carol Ray Nino, 1999. Slab-built with oxides and glazes, fired to 1300°C. 23 × 34 × 8.5cm (9 × 13 × 3in). Photo David Mingot.

ANNE LIGHTWOOD works with a material which could be described either as porcelain or a very fine stoneware, depending on the quantity and grade of molochite added. It is mixed in 68l (15gal) batches in a blunger, and the same basic recipe is used to make coloured porcelain for handbuilding, fine slip for spraying, and the slip to which paper pulp is added. This is her porcelain slip recipe:

Grolleg china clay	45%
Hyplas 71 ball clay	20%
Feldspar	20%
Quartz	15%
Bentonite	2%
Molochite	up to 5%

This is strained through a 60-mesh sieve for handbuilding, and stains are added, in amounts varying from less than 1 per cent for blues, to 10 per cent for pinks and yellows; these have first been mixed with water to make them liquid and easy to blend. The resulting coloured slips are further screened through a 120 mesh if they are to be sprayed, or dried out on plaster batts if they are to be used in the plastic state. For

'*Landscape Platter*' by Anne Lightwood, 1998. The central area is porcelain paperclay with coloured slip decoration, and the wide edges are stoneware paperclay containing iron. Approximately 42 × 42cm (16 × 16in).

paperclay, two or three jugs of slip, depending on the type of work to be made, are combined with one of pulp made from newsprint. Coloured slip can be used, but is expensive on stain, and colours are more usually achieved by spraying layers onto the surface. Pieces are frequently only once-fired, to a temperature of 1260°C.

Wali Hawes Dragon Kiln
4 parts paper pulp (recycled newsprint)
6 parts coarse clay (local Japanese mountain clay)
1 part grog
The water content of the prepared paperclay was 38%.
The optimum firing temperature of this particular clay is 1100°C.

Once any of these bodies has been fired it will behave like the clay it was originally composed from, the only difference being that it is more porous, the degree depending upon the quantity of fibre. The greater the amount of fibre, the more porous the body, even at stoneware temperatures.

Glazes are used by paperclay potters, but these seem of much less interest than other treatments such as staining with oxides and prepared colours, coating with slips, or post-firing smoking. It is reasonable to suppose that any glaze found satisfactory for the original clay will also suit the paperclay version, and since many glaze recipes are already published, they have not been included here. Details of special treatments are given alongside illustrations of the work.

> **Tip**
>
> Sieves are graded by mesh size: the coarsest is 60, meaning 60 strands to the inch, and 200 is the finest. If a very coarse or lumpy material is to be sieved it is easier to do it twice, starting with a coarse mesh size, then using a finer size for the second screening.

6 The Dundee Tests

This series of tests was carried out by Claire Brown, a technical assistant in the Ceramics Department of Duncan of Jordanstone College of Art, a faculty of the University of Dundee. Claire has been using paperclay in her own work for several years.

Materials

The clay chosen was porcelain, since this seemed to be the type most used both by students and by those responding to the survey. The clay slip was made by blending in the proportion of 1kg (2.2lb) dry powdered HF porcelain to 465ml (1 pint) water. To this was added a selection of commercially prepared materials sold as additions for clay bodies: these were cellulose, newsprint, diced cotton and denim, all organic fibres, plus polyester and nylon which are man-made. The organic fibres were added to water to make the pulp, 100g (3.53oz) dry material to 1.1l (2pt) water, and in all cases the water was soaked up easily, with little or no surplus to be squeezed out later.

Cellulose and Newsprint

Both of these come shredded very finely so they are light and fluffy in texture; it is a good idea to wear a mask when handling them. They should be put into water immediately, after which there is no problem with dust so long as the bag containing them is kept firmly closed. They blend well, absorbing water easily and mixing evenly, though after mixing there was found to be no appreciable difference between hand-torn and commercially shredded paper as far as handling was concerned; the real difference was in the speed of mixing.

Cotton and Denim Fabric

These fabrics are diced into tiny squares, which take longer to absorb the water. It is important at this point to make sure that they are thoroughly saturated, and not lying in clumps in the bottom of the bucket. Once soaked through they mix without difficulty, but they do tend to sink if this is not the case. A mix containing them must be well stirred before use, particularly if it has been standing for any length of time. The texture of the threads remains in the clay after firing, giving a chunky effect unless the surface is rolled.

Ratios: The materials were added to the clay slip in four ratios:

1/1 – clay and pulp in equal volume;
2/1 – twice the volume of clay to pulp;
3/1 – three times; and
4/1 – four times the volume of clay to pulp.

Nylon and Polyester Fibres

These were cut into short lengths of about 1cm (½in) or less. They are non-porous, and would therefore be suspended within a slip mix, needing constant stirring to keep them evenly distributed. For this reason they were wedged by hand into plastic clay in three ratios: 1g, 2g and 3g dry fibre to 1kg (2.2lb) clay. Little difference was found in the handling properties between the highest and lowest amounts added, and only small variations were noted in the final firing results.

The apparent difference in the quantities of fibres added is explained by the fact that the organic materials were added wet, by volume, while the man-made ones were added dry, by weight.

A group of bisqued tiles in the kiln, propped by the corners to test warping. (All the photos in this section are by Claire Brown.)

Tiles

The various mixes were dried and, when sufficiently stiffened, were cut into tiles each measuring 108 mm sq (4.5in sq) and 10mm (0.04in) thick, then fired in an electric kiln to 1000°C, for bisque, followed by one batch at 1100°C, and others at 1240°C and 1280°C, the highest temperature tested. None of the tiles was glazed.

Shrinkage was measured, and a batch was also tested for warping by being supported only on the corners and fired to top temperature. A further group was tested for absorbency by being placed upright in a bath of vegetable food dye. The tiles were all pressure-tested on an Instron 1196 machine to check both the strength of unfired green ware, and that at 1280°C, the top temperature tested.

Tip
For curved shapes, paperclay can be cut with scissors, providing it is not too hard.

In all cases three tests were done and an average taken. It was not possible to do more because of constraints of time and cost, and three was considered to be the minimum to give a fair result. The control was the same HF porcelain as that used for the various mixes. One or two rogue results can be explained by the slightly empiric testing methods carried out in the workshop rather than in a laboratory; however, the aim was always to establish general guidelines of use to potters, rather than to produce a scientific treatise. The results are shown in the accompanying graphs and photographs (*see* overleaf), and were surprising, mainly in the uniformity they showed and the small percentage differences noted, both between the materials used and the volumes added.

Tip
Paperclay blunts tools, and may not cut easily with a knife because of the fibres pulling; but thin, soft sheets of paperclay can easily be torn to size by holding a ruler or straight edge on the sheet, and pulling a strip away from it. Stiffer, leather-hard sheets can be scored on the back, then turned over and the sheet split by bending it over the edge of the table. Both these methods give a pleasing soft edge, rather than a hard cut one; but they only work for straight edges.

Shrinkage

With each of the fibres added, in whatever proportion, shrinkage was very small from wet to dry – between 2 and 3 per cent (the control was 4.5). This was still true after firing to a bisque temperature of 1000°C when the figure (at all ratios) was 3–4 per cent, and the control was 5 per cent. However, it appeared that over 1000°C, the higher temperature the greater the shrinkage, until at 1280°C (the highest tested) there was little difference between the control at 15 per cent and the fibre clays at around 14 per cent. Newsprint showed up worst in all tests, the shrinkage (16 per cent) being actually greater than that of the control at top temperature, in whichever proportion used.

Warping

The results here were also remarkably consistent, with only a slight curve on the corners when the tiles were balanced on kiln props and fired to 1280°C. However, this would not necessarily be the case with larger or thinner clay sheets; the tiles used for experiment were quite small and relatively thick for their size: when laid flat there was no measurable warping, making the material potentially very useful for murals and wall panels. Again there was little difference between the different fibres, or between the proportions used.

Absorbency

Tiles which had been fired to 1280°C were propped in a bath of food colouring so that the lower edge was just submerged. In most cases the results were instantaneous, with the dye being immediately sucked into the clay. In this case the quantity of fibre did make a noticeable difference and, as might be expected, those containing the greatest amount were the most porous. The dye also appeared to be drawn up to the top of the

*T*ile pieces placed in a bath of food dye to test absorbency. Results were dramatic, those containing the highest ratio of fibre being the most absorbent.

GRAPH 1. *Force (Kn) Required to Break the Various Unfired Tiles.*

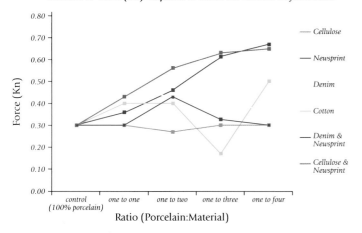

GRAPH 2. *Force (Kn) Required to Break the Various Unfired Tiles.*

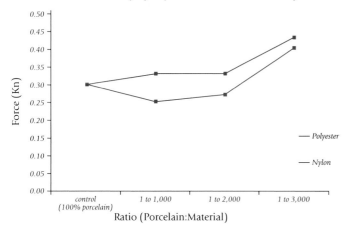

piece so that the colour on that edge was intensified. The control was vitreous and stayed white, while both nylon and polyester remained white at the top, showing that it took longer for moisture to penetrate the body. The check was only by eye and a rough linear measurement, but a similar test could be done more precisely, weighing the amount absorbed and noting the time taken to reach measured marks, and this would be necessary if the work was required to be weatherproof.

Flexion Test

This was done to assess the relative strengths of the materials at difference pressure – as unfired green ware, and after firing to top temperature. The measurement was in Kilonewtons per square metre, and the pressure was increased until the tile broke.

Unfired tiles containing fibre were considerably stronger than the control and could be pressed back together and repaired, while the porcelain crumbled at a lesser pressure. Mixed fibres – cellulose and newsprint, and denim with newsprint – were nearly twice as strong as the control at

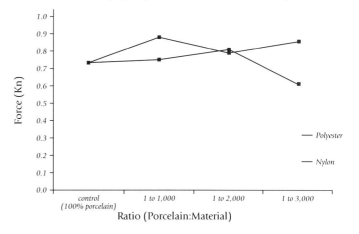

this point, and polyester and nylon considerably better (*see* Graphs 1 and 2).

At 1280°C, polyester and nylon were also stronger than the control when used in ratio 1:1,000 and 1:2,000, and nylon remained stronger at 1:3,000, but the tiles containing the organic fibres were actually weaker than the control, all breaking below the control figure, no matter what the fibre ratio (*see* Graphs 3 and 4). This was a considerable surprise, since the theory is very strongly held by makers that paperclay is in all cases stronger, the gaps left in the structure when fibres burn out acting as lacunae similar to the cavities in bone. (These lighten the weight, particularly in birds, but also help to stop fractures, as the break occurs in the dense material, but stops and does not run across the gap.)

This would not seem to be the case with clay, however. It is measurably stronger with fibre additions at lower temperatures, allowing very different structures to be built, but increasingly less so as the temperature rises, so that at high temperatures the work becomes fragile. Other additions as well as fibre are necessary for strength.

GRAPH 4. Force (Kn) Required to Break the Various Tiles (Fired at 1280°C).

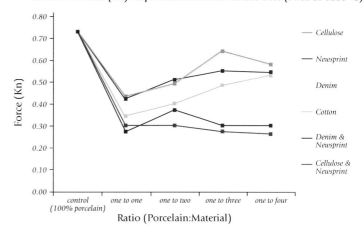

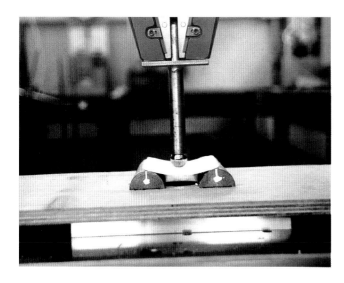

*P*ressure machine (above) *and tiles after tests* (right). *Results are shown in the accompanying graphs.*

A group of thrown cylinders drying out. The texture of the fibres can be seen clearly, particularly the threads of blue denim in the chunky one. The control is on the left, and the cellulose in the centre.

The cylinders after firing. Those shown are the denim group. The control is on the left, and the ratios are 1:4, 1:3, 1:2 and 1:1, fibre to clay.

Different clays contain a variety of ingredients including grog, and it seems that a blend is most satisfactory, as is a mixture of fibres both organic and man-made, with the inclusion of grog for larger work.

It is significant that many makers have already realized these factors, and the number who raku fire, or who smoke at low temperatures, as well as those deliberately making fragile, precious pieces, clearly recognize these qualities.

Throwing

As an additional experiment, the same materials were tested for their throwing potential by Sean Kingsley, ceramics assistant in the same department. The clay was weighed into 500g (1.1lb) balls, and similar cylinders were thrown to see what height each different blend could reach. The fine cellulose was found to be the best of the organic fibres, and when used in a small proportion (one to four) it actually improved the feel of the clay. This blend could also be turned, and though the fibres pulled a little, it was possible to compress the surface smooth again. The main benefit appeared to be reducing the stickiness of the clay so that the turnings fell away cleanly without snagging on the body. One factor which had not been anticipated was that after firing to 1,280°C the blend containing cellulose was quite discernibly whiter and brighter than the pure porcelain control, looking almost as though the sample had been given a coating of tin glaze. The higher the percentage of cellulose, the whiter the body, the difference showing as graphically as a demonstration in a detergent advertisement – though it is not really possible to reproduce this clearly in a photograph.

Nylon and polyester also threw relatively well, but were not turned because the fibres snagged and caught on tools. Denim was the least satisfactory, impossible to throw at the highest ratio, and very lumpy, as was to be expected. The cotton squares were better, but there is little point in adding this type of fibre to a body meant for throwing.

None of the cylinders was able to be thrown as thin or as tall as the control, the man-made fibres coming closest. The cylinders were brushed with oxide and dipped in transparent glaze, then fired in the same temperature ranges. They seemed to absorb a larger amount of glaze than normal, bearing out the results seen in the absorbency tests, but there were no problems or further surprises.

Casting

To complete the series of tests, some of the slips were cast in a plaster mould with sharp edges to test the degree of precision that could be achieved; the photograph illustrates the results. Again, the fine cellulose was by far the most satisfactory, giving crisp lines with a dense, smooth surface, and lifting easily from the mould. There was difficulty with the lumpier slips, which settled out so that the bottom was thick and chunky and nothing had adhered to the side walls; but as can be seen, even this has its possibilities once the factor is known.

The set of casts before firing; the sharpest is that containing cellulose fibre. Others from left to right are newsprint, diced cotton and denim.

One extra material was added for fun, though it is not likely to be in general circulation: shredded bank notes! Some sacks of them had been donated to the college, but sadly the paper proved of too special a quality and did not break down satisfactorily, involving far more effort than it was worth.

Many of those whose work appears in this book use straw or other fibres to achieve very specific results, the broken textures creating sculptural effect. Such individual experimentation is to be encouraged, but cannot be tested very accurately. As always, it is the experience of materials and firing techniques which counts, and there are not many short cuts to that.

7 Elements of Change

To non-potters the name 'paperclay' seems a contradiction in terms, since paper is fragile and burns away, while clay after firing is hard and permanent. One of the main factors that has made the development of paperclay possible is the recent advance in papermaking technology which has resulted in the corresponding abundance, variety and cheapness of papers now available everywhere.

Papermakers have known about clay for a very long time, using it as a filler to plug the gaps between pulped and broken-down fibres. China clay is used extensively in the paper industry for coating papers which are used for colour printing in particular. Though many additives have been mixed with clays, depending on the purpose for which they are to be used, it has taken a long time for potters to turn to paper.

Rauschenberg and the Gemini Project in India

Throughout the sixties, experimental approaches to papermaking were made by artists using paper in a sculptural way, particularly in America. One of those involved was artist Robert Rauschenberg, who, in 1974, made a successful visit to a traditional papermill in France, where he produced a series of papers incorporating coloured tissues. In the following year he went to India. He was invited to Ahmedabad, a textile-making centre and the birthplace of Mahatma Gandhi, by a wealthy family who were well educated and familiar with Western ideas, particularly American art of the period. Rauschenberg was dedicated to breaking with tradition, and had been using innovative two- and three-dimensional processes to combine printmaking and sculpture. He chose to go to India because of the unique skills involving papermaking and fabric to be found there.

One of Gandhi's ideals had been to set up *ashrams* or training centres, where the lowest caste of untouchables could learn a variety of traditional craft skills and be able to earn enough to improve their lives. Rauschenberg worked on one of these ashrams for a month, with a good labour force but few technical resources. There was a desire to show that art could be open to all, but no intention to set up any long-term project.

Rauschenberg used what he called 'rag mud', a combination of paper pulp and the adobe clay used locally for building. The adobe mixture included spices such as fenugreek and tamarind seed, traditionally believed to be insect repellent, and ground chalk, powdered gum and copper sulphate. The rag mud was hand-moulded into sculptural shapes about 3.7–7.6cm (1.5–3in) thick and incorporating rope, twine, bamboo and coloured silks. The work was never designed to be fired, but because of the high humidity it could not be left to dry naturally even in temperatures approaching 100°C: it had to be dried quickly until all the moisture had evaporated, and for this it was put in the ovens that were normally used for drying screened fabrics. Even if left damp only overnight, mildew would develop, quickly followed by infestations of insects and sometimes an overpowering smell of decay. During the period of the Gemini project, as it was known, two series of works – 'Bones' and 'Unions' – were made, and prototypes developed for six further editions. This would seem to be the first documented use of paperclay for purely artistic purposes.

'Moulin Moule' by Carol Farrow, mid-1980s. Paper made from cotton linters cast in situ on wood and stone; painted and waxed. 102 × 190cm (40 × 75in).

Paperclay in Wales

The first introduction to paperclay for many potters in Great Britain must have been in 1993 when Brian Gartside carried bone-dry sheets of paperclay in a suitcase from his home in New Zealand to an international potters' festival in Wales. In a wonderful, lighthearted performance showing great technical skill and understanding of the material, he first produced the rigid sheets with a flourish from the real suitcase. Then (by magic, it almost seemed) in a very short time he assembled the slabs into a paperclay suitcase complete with handle – which he bore proudly off stage *by the handle!* This was a tribute to the material – but equally to his nerve. At another demonstration he tore up toilet rolls and mixed them in a dustbin with a paint mixer attachment on an electric drill before adding clay to make a paperclay slip in what we would now describe as the normal way. It seemed crazy at the time.

Articles written by Brian describing his method for making paperclay, and setting out some of the advantages of the material, were published first in New Zealand and later in 1994 in *Ceramic Review*. Illustrated with step-by-step photographs, these spread the news of paperclay even wider.

Rosette Gault is often credited with being the 'discoverer' of paperclay, and indeed she gave a paper at a conference in Finland in 1992 describing the properties of the revolutionary new material which she had been researching in detail. She also spoke at a conference called 'Playing with Fire', held in London in 1994. These brought the knowledge of paperclay into more general public discussion, and information spread throughout the potting world.

It is a strange phenomenon that individuals working on their own in different countries seem to make similar discoveries at much the same time. This happened with the use of stains and colours in clay a few years ago, and is now the case with paperclay. Practitioners developing the material had been working individually as far apart as America, Finland and New Zealand, and although articles appeared worldwide scattered through various ceramics magazines, Rosette Gault can be credited with being the first to collate and publish her research in book form, thus making the possibilities of paperclay even more widely known. To students in many colleges today, paperclay is just an alternative type of clay, and working with it, or other additives, has become quite routine. In her book she mentions that others were working along similar lines as far back as the seventies, but it was a spell at an artist's residence at Banff in Canada in 1990 that allowed her to carry out research in much greater depth, and also to meet other international artists spending time there. For her, this proved to be a time of great excitement and inspiration.

'To D.B....this story will never end' by Carol Farrow, late 1970s. Book-fired to 1300°C, on slipcast ceramic base including sawdust; raku fired. Photo Stephen Harper.

The Influence of Goldsmith's

Already in London, throughout the seventies and eighties, a similarly high-powered group of students, whose work has since become internationally known, was working in the Ceramics Department at Goldsmith's College. Among them was post-graduate ceramics student **CAROL FARROW**, who was at that time experimenting with firing many materials other than clay. One of those materials was paper.

'Country Life' by Carol Farrow, early 1980s. Saggar-fired book, bound rolled magazine also fired to 1300°C, mounted on oiled slate base.

Carol discovered that the high proportion of china clay in the coated papers used for glossy magazines would leave what she described as 'a very fragile ceramic material' when fired to the exceedingly high temperature of around 1300°C. These visual and physical properties interested her and, in an article published in *Artists' Newsletter* in 1987, she describes how she began to bind up stacks of books or magazines with stainless-steel wire to restrain them and prevent them opening up during firing. She also enclosed them in saggars or weighted them down with kiln furniture to achieve a transformation completely at odds with the more usual utilitarian aspect of fired clay. Knowing how the different papers reacted at varying temperatures

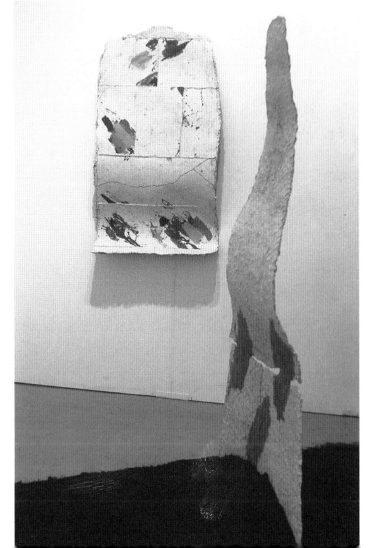

*T*wo paperclay slabs by Carol Farrow, late 1970s. Made with a 50–50 mix of T-material and cotton linters buttered onto plaster slabs already painted with underglaze colour; lifted when dry and fired upright to 1300°C. Piece on wall 1.5m (5ft) high, front one 1.8m (6ft), made in three sections and joined using fibreglass coated with sand. Front piece standing in sand.

was crucial, as was control of the kiln. The resulting pieces were so fragile it was difficult even to lift them from the kiln, but Carol liked the feeling that their transitory qualities echoed the equally transitory nature of much of today's written matter.

Books are considered to be objects of virtue and wisdom, but the question being posed was to what degree they had become merely mementos of past experience, or status symbols to be stored on our shelves, often without even being read, let alone re-read. The firing transformed them, giving another life, albeit a very brief one. The element of change was integral in considering each piece.

This spell of experimentation resulted in a greater knowledge of the behaviour of different types of manufactured papers, and the next logical step was to make handmade paper and add clay to this. Very soon Carol began mixing well-pulped cotton linters or ordinary (non-china clay) papers with clay slurry, and trying out different proportions of pulp to clay. The resulting mix was sometimes dried on a plaster bat, or alternatively spread as a thin surface on to paper or card. With a 50/50 mix of pulp and clay she found it was possible to make large, thin sheets up to 1.5m (5ft) high that had sufficient green strength to allow them to be transported around the studio and into the kiln in a way which would simply not have been possible without the fibre content. A denser surface was achieved by using a ratio of seventy parts clay to thirty of pulp.

With this amount of paper the surface tends to be slightly rough and pitted, and the body is porous even after a high firing; but this quality is enhanced, and sometimes even emphasized, by sawdust smoking.

Firing Large Sheets

Both material and kiln were frequently tested to the limits of their capacity, taking the firings as high as the kiln could reach, even well above the recommended temperature for the clay body. Under such extreme conditions, firing flat is the best option for smaller pieces, but this is not possible in most kilns when the work is on a large scale. Firing very large sheets without too much distortion posed problems which were overcome by building a staggered wall of kiln bricks within the kiln. The wall incorporated air spaces, allowing the heat to circulate. The clay sheets were placed upright against this, and if several were to be fired together, a thin layer of ceramic fibre was placed between each piece. A second, similar wall was then built as close against the sheets as possible to restrict movement and the risk of slumping. The firing schedule was followed as normal, except the kiln was slowed down at around 250°C, when a great deal of smoke would be released from the burning paper. This way of working was a revolutionary approach at the time.

Carol has continued working with both paper and paperclay, depending on the availability of a kiln, and in making pieces on a large scale; she currently works in London and France.

Burning Books

In Japan at about the same time, Yohei Nishimura was studying ceramics: although he considered himself to be a sculptor, he studied ceramics because of his interest in the firing process, and because of his belief that firing wipes away traces of technique which sculpture leaves behind. In his work using fired books, no additional clay was applied to them before they were subjected to temperatures of around 1000°C. The paper is reduced to ashes and collapses when burned, and the tension between fire and paper appears, the fire becoming another material. The book retains a hint of its form even as it becomes a ruin, but after firing the message it has contained is wiped out.

'Ruins of books, non-existent books.' The fired books pose questions about forms of existence, not 'What is art?' but 'What generates significance in art?'

Crossing the Boundaries

Today it would seem there are few rules that cannot be broken, and no boundaries which cannot be crossed. Many artists trained in other media are turning to clay because they enjoy its spontaneity and vitality, and are prepared to accept its frequent unpredictability. With such an open attitude they come to the material free from preconceptions, and being unaware of many of the possible pitfalls, are not afraid to push materials deliberately to their limits. New techniques are evolved to deal with new problems or to express original ideas, and artists are not held back by traditions from the past.

What is important, however, is that as artists develop their own language, they also provide clues to the onlooker as to how to view the work. 'Form follows function'

Fired Book by Hazel Thomson, 1996. Porcelain casting slip pasted over photocopied paper and fired to 1260°C; traces of print can still be seen. The fragility is deliberate, posing the question of whether the piece can be handled.

is no longer a useful adage when the function is to rouse the imagination or to evoke emotion or disturb sensibilities, so the maker must ensure that the viewer can understand enough of the particular language to decipher the message he or she is proclaiming.

'Closing the Gap – making ends meet' by Graham Hay, 1996. Unfired stoneware paperclay. 84 × 84 × 18cm (33 × 33 × 7in). Photo Victor France.

New Ways of Thinking

It is hard to imagine how **GRAHAM HAY** could make his incredible pieces without paperclay, and the qualities of the material have influenced both his thinking and the way in which he works. In the dry heat of western Australia clay dries quickly, and components for his sculptures are allowed to dry out completely before they are joined with paperclay slip to make his complex constructions. He calls this wet-and-dry technique 'dip 'n stick'. If changes need to be made it is easy to soak an area and break or cut it off; and just as easily new areas can be added dry to dry and held together with slip; or plastic paperclay can be added to dry. This increased spontaneity means that unfired work can be pulled apart and rejoined and repeatedly reassembled until a satisfactory result is achieved. For Graham, working in this way has meant an even greater degree of irreverence to the normal conventions of working with clay.

It is hard to describe the work that he makes. It is totally original, fitting into no known category and not seeming to come from any recognizable ceramic tradition, but rather to derive from the way in which animal structures are built. It includes elements which appear to be taken from partly eroded anthills, or coral reefs, or papery wasps' nests chewed from old wood, which look delicate but are actually very strong. To a northern Scot such as I am, his work seems to epitomize the land from which it comes: an alien continent in a different hemisphere, full of heat and light, space and sudden flashes of intense colour.

But Graham describes his work as being concerned with people and the organizations and institutions they create or are drawn into, the mass of tiny units that build up to make the whole great edifice. The titles of the works reflect this: *Blooming Bureaucracy*, or *City Hall* for instance. While architectural elements are used as metaphors, the building is never as rigid as it appears, and '... buildings are not the organizations, people are, and they regularly change'. Our social status is frequently defined by our job or the position we hold within a group, and there are tensions both within and outside the circle. The paperless office is a myth, and the huge amounts of paper generated even in the computer age are another concern, making paperclay a particularly suitable medium '...because paper is a constant companion in the creation and maintenance of organizations and institutions'. Some recent work has been made entirely from paper.

Before using paperclay Graham had difficulties in making tall or top-heavy work, and found the process of propping large pieces and controlling drying to avoid cracking too tedious, putting a restriction on the freedom of expression that he wanted to convey. Now, because of paperclay's rapid drying, he finds it is possible to build in all directions, so that within a dry rod framework building can be up, down or sideways, inwards or outwards in planes, rods or spheres. This type of structure breaks away from the conventional vessel or wall, so that the gaps and spaces giving glimpses to the interior or beyond are as important as the solid elements. Graham describes this as being akin to a three-dimensional drawing in space, with the lines having real mass rather than being merely an illusion.

Always an innovator, he has developed unorthodox methods of creating the components that he wants for his pieces. Paperclay sheets are thinned by throwing them repeatedly on the ground, always the same way up; this also gives a roughened, earthy texture to one side of the clay. Texture and surface detail are important in his work, and the hardness of dry paperclay means that it is not blurred in subsequent handling and assembling. The sheets can then be torn up into smaller pieces for stacking or assembling.

Rods are made by dipping wool or cotton (or even spaghetti!) into paperclay slip and allowing them to dry till stiff. Like making a candle from molten wax, the cord must be dipped several times to achieve sufficient thickness; it must also be dried out thoroughly between each dip, or the previous layer will not be sufficiently absorbent to take up more slip. This is a much easier way to achieve long, straight rods than trying to roll coils evenly, and because the fibres in the paperclay pull and catch, using an extruder is not satisfactory either.

Curved shapes can be made by draping plastic sheets or rods over a former, and tapered rods can be made from plastic clay curved or bent into spirals when soft, then assembled when stiff enough. Sometimes pasta is mixed into the slip, and after firing the surface can be opened up, giving a broken 'anthill' effect. All the components are made individually and dried before being joined and fired. This gives great flexibility, and it also means that any extra pieces can be stored until needed and used even months later in other work.

In a wonderful piece of lateral thinking, Graham suggests that the incredible strength of unfired paperclay could revolutionize the way that artists exhibit and communicate. Instead of having to pay the considerable expenses of sending delicate fired objects from one country to another, why not send *unfired* components to local artists who could assemble and fire them, even adding embellishments of their own as they thought fit? That would truly introduce a real element of change.

'Reach' by
Graham Hay, 1999.
Earthenware
paperclay. 60 × 23 ×
20cm (24 × 9 × 8in).
Photo Victor France.

8 Layers and Laminations

'Last Thoughts' by Helen Smith, 1998. Part of an installation entitled 'Forgotten Seas'. Bowls are moulded from the cast of a skull, the interior layer printed, then after firing boiled with saline solution to become encrusted with crystals of salt. The work carries allusions to the Last Supper, to an operating table, or more simply to an archivist's cataloguing bench.

Layers do not have to be in physical form only: many makers describe being interested in, or inspired by, the process of accretion, where layers of meaning are gradually built up and ascribed to particular objects, thus adding a significance beyond their original function. Others are moved by the opposite – where slow decay or disintegration gradually sheds layers, peeling them away so that the object reveals hidden secrets, until finally it is reduced to the dust from which it came. Many have described finding inspiration in the work of past generations and in the clues to lost cultures deciphered from the relics and shards preserved in museum cases. In either case the onlooker is invited to participate. The willingness of the viewer to enter the world of the artist's imagination is vital to the understanding of the work, just as it may be with a painting or sculpture; indeed, without such involvement and readiness to enter a dialogue, much of the content of the piece will be lost. Each viewer will come with his own agenda and will be moved, or otherwise, by different aspects, so the work will come to assume a whole variety of meanings to every audience. This is one real test of its quality.

Ceramics combines the characteristics of both painting and sculpture. The surface quality of the clay is often beguiling, with colours and mark-making which resemble painting or drawing, yet which ask to be touched in a way not permissible with 'flat' art. Layers of glaze, each with a slightly different characteristic, one reacting with another and hiding or revealing impressions below, give a depth and quality particular to ceramics and not achievable in any other medium. For many ceramic artists, the tactile quality of the ceramic surfaces they make is an important factor – but form is of equal importance, the three-dimensional nature of the objects giving them their sculptural value. Linking these aspects in a balanced, satisfying whole is an overriding consideration for most potters.

Creating the Layers

HAZEL THOMSON is concerned with boundaries, and the question of how easy it is to 'cross the line' and intrude on another's 'space'. She feels that the fragility of the material and the thinness of the sheets represent this dilemma, and emphasizes the difficulties we face in deciding how far to go. The actual layered pieces were made after studying drystone dykes in Cornwall, where the structure is built up by placing the stone or slate at right-angles to the ground.

Methods and Materials

Like many others, Hazel tried a variety of both clays and papers before she found the combination she preferred. She discarded newsprint as being too dull and lifeless, considering that it added little to the quality of the body, and in this, many others agreed with her – although her choice of a glossy coated paper from a printers is not one that many have found satisfactory. However, Hazel found that this particular paper – which she believes contains a high proportion of china clay in its coating – had extraordinary effects: first, it enabled her to achieve very subtle yellow colours, and it also produced shiny patches in the clay after firing. This was important, since it did not seem worth making additions unless they left their mark behind. Much of Hazel's work is laminated, using casting slip mixed with this high quality paper which gives sufficient strength to the clay to prevent warping.

'Enclosure' by Hazel Thomson. Laminated clay structure with paper and porcelain casting slip. The work explores boundaries, and how easy it is to overstep the line and intrude on another's space. The fragility adds to the uncertainty.

In Switzerland, **URSULA KUPFER** has also developed her own laminating technique for large-scale platters and bowls. She makes three or four different coloured clays, and dries each in sheets about 2cm (¾in) thick on separate plaster batts. When the sheets are stiff enough to be handled, but before they are quite leather hard, she cuts them into strips approximately 1–2cm (⅜–¾in) wide and presses these together, using a little slurry if necessary. The different colours are combined in various ways, depending on the project.

Bowls are made in moulds, or a sand bed is used for very large pieces; these are formed quite spontaneously, with clay being added whenever and wherever the form seems to need it, even when the dish is dry. Further manipulation by tearing, pressing, squeezing or scratching may also be done before bisque firing. Sometimes the second firing is in a specially built, brick kiln in the garden where the dishes are smoked with either sawdust or shavings. Vermiculite soaked in a solution of metallic salts such as copper or iron sulphate may sometimes be placed in the dishes to add extra colour, or they may be filled with sand to resist the smoke in certain areas.

Previous work with agate ware and an interest in surfaces led **KATHY SHADWELL** to laminating, using a whole variety of clays from porcelain to crank. For her, the interest lay in the response between the different clays. The agate clay is made by adding stains or oxides to a porcelain body. Her method is to texture quite a thick sheet of T-material with brushes, knives or cloths, and then to lay strips or small sections of prepared agate clay onto it. The whole plastic slab is then stretched into thinner sheets, which are sometimes further impressed before they are used to build with. The colour and patterning thus become quite random, though there is obviously considerable choice in the way they are assembled. Kathy describes the process as being like taking a blank sheet of paper and covering it with abstract marks.

ZOE HALL is another potter who uses two very disparate materials: she works with both brick clay and porcelain combined with paper pulp, although not both in the same piece at the same time. Accrington clay is a local Lancashire clay used for brick-making which has a very coarse, groggy body. Zoe makes this into slip by first drying it out, then grinding it into powder and finally adding it to water until she obtains the consistency she wants. In a high ratio of pulp to clay she then mixes equal quantities of both, and dries the mix in a mould until it reaches a workable plastic consistency. This body is fired to 1020°C.

*F*igure by Kathy
Shadwell, using mixed
clays and agate inlay;
fired to 1260°C in a
gas kiln.

The porcelain body is made in the same way, and using the same proportions of clay slip and pulp, but about 12 per cent silver sand is added to decrease the shrinkage that would otherwise be unacceptably high (Zoe describes it as almost 30 per cent). Coloured slip, dried and crushed to a powdered form, is also sometimes added to the porcelain mix, and this can give bright flashes in the finished work, as long as it is not broken up and blended too smoothly.

Surface pattern, seams and edges are important in Zoe's work, which is also much concerned with lightness and movement. Tearing various papers and contrasting these with smooth surfaces creates the tension she is seeking, and she has an unusual way of achieving this. First the clay is rolled into sheets, fairly thickly, then a template is laid on top and a cut made around it, half way through the thickness of the clay. The top surface of the clay sheet is then torn away from around the template, revealing a textured surface with a torn edge below. Several pieces made in this way are then layered together until the desired depth is reached. An opening made through the layers then links them all together.

Pressed form by Zoe Hall. Porcelain paperclay with coloured inclusions. Layers are made by tearing through the top half of the clay sheet, leaving the surface rough; fired to 1260°C.

Hidden Depths

It is the intention of **FREDERICK PAYNE** to link many hidden elements – both physical and intellectual – in his work. Coming from a house which he describes as being full of paper, and from a family involved with expressing ideas in both words and images (his grandfather was an illustrator, his mother a writer and his father a curator at the Royal Shakespeare Picture Gallery), he continues the family traditions by using his grandfather's lino printing techniques – and sometimes even his blocks – to emboss the surfaces of the clay; he then combines this with the modern material of fibreglass, enclosed within a porcelain slip, to create his own highly original pieces.

His main concern is with light and dark, with the contrasts only truly appreciated when the pieces are lit. The variations in thickness give tonal shading, and also reveal any drawing hidden between the layers. The thinner the porcelain, the more translucent it will be, and the greater the contrast in the embossed areas.

Many of Frederick's ideas come from paper. Bending and folding flat sheets, as in Origami, can create three-dimensional forms of complexity and strength, and cardboard is made even stronger by laminating and corrugating layers. By folding clay sheets into self-supporting geometric shapes, a minimum of clay is used and maximum translucency achieved.

As a child he drew on the back of old posters brought back home by his father, and by holding these to the light the images on both sides could be seen at once. This tied in with later college experiences of glass techniques, when he saw colour being fused

Stacked curved form by Frederick Payne. Thin sheets are embossed, then built up using templates to form folds and curves, and to achieve maximum translucency while using minimum clay. Photo Alan Bye.

within laminated sheets of glass, and strips of glass being melted together. The work of glass engravers such as Laurence Whistler also embraced the idea of one image being seen through another. The engraving on the glass is controlled so that each image is complete in itself, yet all are united, and one image enhances the other as the bowl is turned.

Like many others who go to great lengths to achieve a desired effect, Frederick's method is labour-intensive. Complex pieces are hand built from thin sheets of clay formed by dipping fibreglass tissue into porcelain slip. The tissue is very fine, thinner than normal tissue paper, and dipping is done only once to achieve the greatest possible degree of thinness and translucency. The clay sheets are dried out on plaster slabs until they are leather hard, then burnished smooth with the back of a spoon; after this the sections needed can be cut out and stored damp until required.

To emboss the pieces, they are laid on the lino and the clay is pressed firmly into the block with the fingers. This gives a crisp copy, and any cracks which develop during drying can be sealed by brushing with a little water. The process gives a reverse image. In a normal printing process the lino that has been cut away would be white; here, however, it is the thickest part of the clay and therefore appears darkest in the porcelain. The depth and direction of the cuts can also have considerable importance, since these are shown up by the light. Frequently the images carved on the lino blocks are also printed using white ink on black paper, giving a dramatic effect which echoes the clay piece.

Translucent flower vase by Frederick Payne. Fibreglass within porcelain slip giving very thin sheets which are then embossed and stained. Photo Alan Bye.

Sometimes the ceramic object and the lino-cut print may be exhibited together, giving another dimension to both.

Detail is added by painting raised areas with oxides or high temperature stains after embossing and before covering with another layer of clay: like this the drawing is concealed and does not show until the piece is lit. Coloured panels are sometimes made by adding about 5 per cent of bodystain to the slip before the fibreglass tissue is dipped.

Fibreglass consists of spun and woven strands of silica, which melt and fuse within the clay body, thus becoming an integral part of the structure of the piece; the fact that it does this, rather than burning away, is an important factor in determining its use as an additive.

Along with other potters, Frederick enjoys the ambiguity of the material he creates. It can be folded, embossed and printed on like paper; cut, curved and gathered like fabric; it is translucent like glass; and it can take on the appearance of many other materials, yet has a structural strength and durability entirely its own.

Interior Secrets

HELEN SMITH is another artist who has her own language, hinting at secrets or half-forgotten dreams, and demanding an effort of understanding from the viewer. The titles give a clue, but they are enigmatic and have no fixed interpretation. At first sight the objects seem familiar, and they are frequently very fragile and arranged in cases as in a museum, which is intended to add a layer of curatorial or historical value – as with shards from an archaeological dig, or items dredged from the bottom of the sea.

Her work is essentially abstract: it is not figurative or realistic, but has an anthropomorphic quality that reminds the onlooker of mummies or bandaged limbs or carefully wrapped relics, long hidden away. They are remains, remnants or residues intended as traces of fleeting moments or models of states of mind translated into material form. The associations aroused in the mind of the onlooker may be more disturbing than the physical appearance of the objects themselves.

Paperclay has deliberately been chosen for its ambiguity, and its hybrid nature is an important quality. Paper carries cultural overtones of language and information,

'Token' by Helen Smith, 1998. Textured layers folded round a salt dough former, fired in an electric kiln to 1000°C, then smoked. 23 × 13cm (9 × 5in).

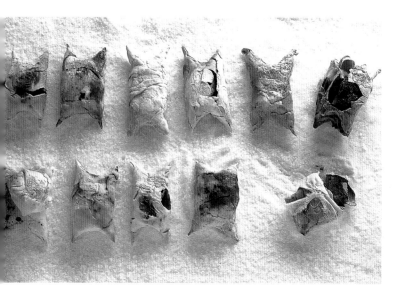

while clay is universal and timeless, less associated with Western thought – although both materials have long been used for communication, as for example in cuneiform clay tablets and papyrus scrolls.

Methods and Materials

Helen uses paperclay like a textile, tearing it into strips, winding, wrapping or pleating, and sometimes rolling muslin or other fabric over the surface to texture it and increase the visual likeness. These qualities are important in her work. Again, she may cast very thin sheets of porcelain paperclay and print on these using a photocopy technique (*described in*

*'P*romises' *(detail) by Helen Smith. Wrapped objects are placed on a bed of salt granules in a glass case. Ceramic pieces are salt glazed, with internal salt-dough former which leaves a cinder residue.*

Chapter 14) before constructing them into other forms. All the pieces for a multiple can be made, printed when convenient and stored until needed because the material can later be re-wetted without risk of cracking. Alternatively the clay may be cast in moulds to make multiples.

For one series entitled 'Last Thoughts', made for a site-specific exhibition, a plaster cast from a human skull was used to make a tableful of what appear at first sight to be simply paper-thin shallow bowls with subtle glaze effects. However, the method used to produce those effects was complex. Each bowl was printed with a sepia portrait by photocopy transfer, and after firing, words – the 'last thoughts' of those portrayed – were written with smoke; finally sea salt was boiled inside, leaving an encrusted, scintillating surface.

Helen's methods of making the pieces are as original as the ideas behind them. She uses porcelain slip and toilet tissue pulp in a ratio of three to one measured by volume for her basic material, which is then wound, wrapped or folded around found objects or specially made formers. The objects have included bones and fruit, and once even the *Yellow Pages* telephone directory, and most burn away leaving only traces of ash or colour; though if metal or wire is incorporated this may remain. Surprisingly the formers are often made from dough, and Helen always uses two specific types. One is simply made from plain flour, water and oil: after firing, a small cinder like charcoal may remain as a shadow within the now hollow form, which is sometimes further reduced by sawdust firing, or smoked using a few sheets of newspaper. The open texture and slight porosity of paperclay lends itself to smoking, since the carbon can penetrate the surface easily. An additional amount of paper is sometimes added to the mix to open the structure even further when work is to be treated in this way.

The other dough contains both salt and bicarbonate of soda, and this must be fired in a salt kiln to avoid damaging either brickwork or the elements of an electric kiln. No additional salt is needed since enough is already included in the dough. Helen calls this 'internal salt glazing', and used the technique for a work she called 'Promises'. In this, copper was also added to the dough or sprinkled onto the former before it was wrapped into a small, parcel-like shape. The firing reduces the copper carbonate giving shaded pinks, a recurring colour in her work.

⑨ Metamorphosis: the Influence of Landscape

The dictionary definition of metamorphosis is 'change of shape, transformation; in folklore as of a human being into a beast, stone, tree etc'. Metamorphic rocks are those formed by the 'alteration of existing rock through heat, pressure or other processes in the earth's crust … by contact with igneous material'. This is actually a fair description of what most potters do: using materials derived from metamorphic rocks, they frequently transform these into simulations of beast, stone or tree bark, using these to express human feelings or emotions, before subjecting the work to the sort of ordeal by fire that produced the original.

It may be the completeness of this circle involving the elements of earth, air, water and fire that potters find satisfying, or the earthiness of their materials, or their durability, but very many describe landscape as a prime source of inspiration even when

'Enclosed Relief' by Roy Ashmore. Detail showing inclusions of pre-fired ceramic pieces, and the effect of combustible material burning away. Earthenware.

they live and work in cities. The underlying structure determining the surface of the land, the visible erosion of rocks by wind or water, the organic forms produced by growth, and the effects of man's habitation, all provide a motivating force for many artists, perhaps because they are elements which cannot be controlled and are only partially understood. There is space left for the imagination.

Creating a Landscape

'Book Page' by Lotte Glob. From an on-going series of works called 'Land/Book/Land' which incorporate many elements experienced in the northern landscape, and include many clay mixtures. This page encloses a fragment of bone.

Traditionally most items made from clay have been hollow, either because they have been thrown on the wheel and are intended to be used as containers, or, if they are sculptures, because the great density of solid clay would weigh far too heavily. More importantly the work would dry out unevenly, resulting in cracking and other technical problems. As the moisture dries from the surface, the outer layer of clay particles shrinks; this increases the tension and causes cracking which may only appear at first as hairline-like markings on the surface, but which may possibly deepen on firing, irrevocably damaging the work.

Damage can also be caused during firing by gases trying to escape from the centre of a thick piece. In the early stages this is likely to be steam, since even work that feels dry to the touch will still contain a certain amount of water. With paperclay this is less of a problem because the tube-like fibres within the clay allow air to penetrate the piece and water to evaporate so that it can dry out more easily, though this still has to be done quite slowly – over days or weeks with really thick pieces. In similar manner, on heating, the cellulose tubes allow those gases that are formed during combustion to escape from within the structure of the piece: thus a solid object may be fired without so much danger of cracking or explosion. However, there will be a considerable release of smoke at about 260°C as the paper in the mix ignites and burns away, and it is as well to slow the kiln at this point, particularly if the piece is large or thick. Gases trapped under the surface of a clay which has vitrified because the temperature has risen too quickly at a critical point – and this point is not always the same: it depends on the composition of the body – can cause the ugly, blister-like appearance known as bloating. Again, this is much less likely with paperclay.

Embracing the Landscape

LOTTE GLOB is Danish, but has lived a large part of her life in Sutherland, the Scottish wilderness at the top of the map of the British Isles. She finds as her inspiration the land and its wildness – the space, the harsh climate, the clear light, the tide on white sand, the action of water and of frost – although rocks are her real passion: 'Rocks, stones, cliffs, boulders come out of the landscape like sculpture, changing always with the light. I spend time watching.'

Lotte's work is rugged, and she has the wonderful idea of returning much of it to the landscape which inspired it, walking miles up mountains to deposit her 'boulders' and other sculptural pieces in crevasses or on mountain tops where only the most intrepid will find them. She calls this 'The Ultimate Rock Garden', and often takes photographs of the results, later exhibiting the photographs alongside her ceramics.

More easily found and appreciated are her 'floating stones': these are sometimes deposited in lochans, but often find their way to garden ponds in more mundane surroundings. They are spheres thrown fairly thinly, turned and altered, then fired (without leaving any aperture) to stoneware temperature using a variety of glazes. They float on water, and when the wind ruffles the surface (all the time in Sutherland) the stones knock gently together with a soothing, slightly tinkling sound.

Almost anything becomes an additive in Lotte's constant experimenting and in her desire to push the boundaries of the possible even further: bitumen from roads, peat and glass, along with sheep's wool, animal skulls and feathers, all are incorporated into sculptural pieces. Currently she is working on a series of 'books' made from printed paperclay, the leaves of which enclose pre-fired pottery pieces, or sometimes whole boulders. These may be pegmatite or granite, but not flint, which explodes. The firing temperature is critical and, knowing her rocks by bitter experience, Lotte aims for 1300 °C or slightly below over a twelve-hour firing cycle, hoping to catch the kiln at exactly the right moment of disintegration when the rock has crumbled open but before it melts completely, and runs out of the kiln.

Book by Lotte Glob. A stoneware book returned to the landscape. Stone inclusion on the 'cover'.

Enclosing a Landscape

ROY ASHMORE describes his work as 'landscapes within the figure': that is, he is using his figurative forms to contain the textures and features of natural landscape, though they may also be seen as suggesting erosion and decay. The pieces contain elements that are both physical and metaphorical. Combustible materials such as hay, sawdust, twigs or grass are mixed with slips to make clay bodies, sometimes apparently containing more fibres than clay content. Oxides are included in the different slips to give varying colours throughout. Making use of paperclay's ability to bond with other materials, Roy might then add pre-fired ceramic shapes or other objects such as old roofing

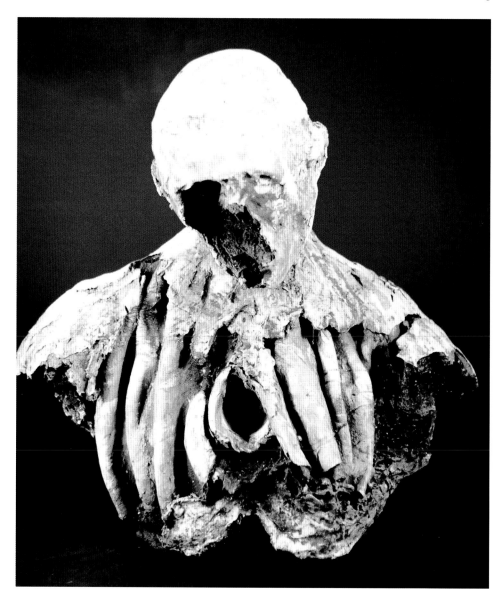

*B*ust by Roy Ashmore. This piece has been made in a mould enclosing pre-fired clay sections with paperclay and straw; after firing, parts are broken away to reveal the interior. Earthenware. 50 × 50cm (20 × 20in).

slates, and these become part of the inner structure of the work and provide interesting textures. This mix is pressed into a mould and allowed to dry out for as long as three to four weeks before firing. The firing creates the desired textures by burning away the fibrous materials and allowing the gases to escape; in this way it is possible to make large forms which are solid, rather than hollow ones requiring an armature.

This sculptural quality allows the piece to be worked on further with chisels or saws after firing, and the problem of the honeycomb-like structure being sometimes rather fragile has been overcome by bisque firing first, then following this with a glaze firing.

To many, the torsos seem to represent death or decaying corpse-like figures rather than landscape, and although the actual surfaces appear more like stone or charred wood or rough tree bark than flesh, this can be disturbing to some viewers. But to Roy, death is as natural and inevitable a process as life itself, and he quotes the North American Indian philosophy that man is not the pinnacle of evolution but part of nature, and no more important in the scheme of things than anything else. We walk over the landscape for a while, maybe scratching its surface, but all civilizations flower and fade. We all return to the land and become part of it in the end.

Eroding the Landscape

CLAUDI CASANOVAS is obsessed with the character of clay itself – its infinite variations and the chaotic state from which it originally emerged, eventually resolved in stability and permanence. His other obsession is with the Catalonian landscape in Spain where he lives, and his work embraces both these concerns energetically, replicating the action of volcanoes or the eroding effects of wind and water. His work is on a large

Textured piece by Claudi Casanovas 1989. Shown at International Potters Festival in Wales. Photo Anne Lightwood.

scale, laminated slabs or platters resembling caverns, cliff faces or the stony landscape which have inspired them. Metal and oxides are included within the body as well as combustible materials such as maize stalks, straw, dung, flour and rice, and when the latter burn away they leave negative spaces which may be further worn down by sand-blasting. Believing that 'there is an engineering solution to every problem', Claudi devises special equipment to enable him to work on a large scale and handle huge pieces. (His unique mould-making methods are described in Chapter 13.) 'Glazing' can involve pouring melted magma from a crucible at high temperature into a series of stoneware 'bowls' and firing them – more like a foundry than a pottery. These vessels may be as much as 120cm (43in) in diameter, and 90cm (35in) high, deriving from the storage vessels known as 'cossi' used in northern Spain. They are built in layers of many differing bodies so that one reacts with the other, and the inside may be reduced while the outside remains oxidized. The pieces are large so to remove them from the human scale and the maker's individuality.

But however dramatic the work or the means of creating it, nothing can compete with the original. The colours and textures will never surpass those of nature, and 'a primitive force explodes in every particle of clay'.

Traces of Landscape

At first sight the work of **TONY FRANKS** appears to have little in common with that of the artists already described in this chapter, but he is another for whom landscape is deeply significant. It provides a constant underlying inspiration for his work, though this may not be immediately obvious on first consideration. Tony was a geographer first, then trained as a designer, and has been known internationally as a potter for many years. All the elements of his first occupations can be detected in his work: it is full of paradox.

His pieces are architectural and precisely controlled and constructed, while still being concerned with the forces of nature. They are cerebral and intellectual, though they still make an appeal to deep human emotions – in particular man's link to the earth. The surfaces are meticulously ground,

'Climbing Idzholm Hill' by Tony Franks, 1998. Vitreous bone china with bracken and grass from Idzholm Hill, fired to 1200°C, ground, sandblasted, coloured with underglaze stains, and refired to 1220°C. 50 × 50 × 35cm (20 × 20 × 14in) high. Photo Shannon Tofts.

*'Glenisla Spring'
by Tony Franks, 1998.
Press-moulded vitreous
bone china with peat
and ferns, fired to
1200°C, sandblasted
outside, coloured with
vanadium pentoxide
outside, rutile inside,
cobalt chloride rim,
fired to 1220°C,
ground and polished.
35cm (14in) diameter,
25cm (10in) high.
Photo Shannon Tofts.*

machined or sandblasted, but his concern is as much with underlying structures as with the outward appearance. Though the work is not very large, the pieces have a certain monumental quality, appearing to take up more space than they actually physically occupy. They need room to be considered.

While maintaining an almost classical outward calm, each piece is imbued with a sense of danger. Large heavy slabs sit, almost appearing suspended, on narrow edges, or solid bowl forms balance on sloping base slabs: there is a feeling of energy only just controlled. The pieces are sculptural, frequently combining a number of elements, and angular slabs or bases with curves cut from them are juxtaposed with hollow vessels which tilt or lie at an angle.

Rims and edges on the bowls are crucially important. Sometimes they may be machined flat and are almost mathematically even, on others a textured crinkly lip will overhang the inner surface, slightly protecting the interior and suggesting the crater of a volcano.

Bone china, the material frequently chosen, is notoriously difficult to work with. Other potters generally use it very thin and light for its translucent qualities, but these pieces are thick and solid: they have actual weight as well as suggesting it. Varying quantities of many different organic materials, unchopped and only roughly crushed or graded, are mixed into whichever body is being used. It is the choice of these materials which is crucial. The concern is not to imitate the places from which the materials originated, but to evoke in the onlooker memories of landscape, ideas aroused by remembered images from rock or hill or cliff face. For this reason materials from specific sites are deliberately selected for each piece, and the title of the work identifies the origins. Several different materials, though all from the same site – leaves, pine needles, mosses, heather, twigs or wood shavings – may be combined in whatever proportion seems to fit the work in mind.

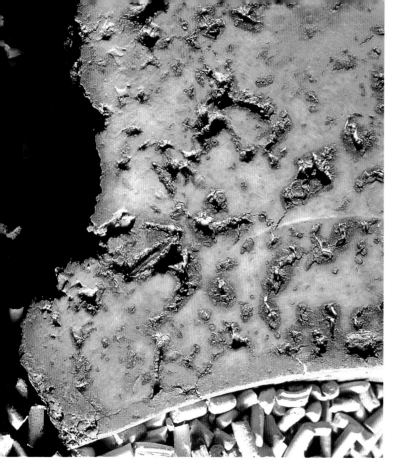

*C*urve/Cove by Tony Franks, 1999. Detail showing surface texture from inclusion of seaweed and leaves, and colour from vanadium pentoxide and titanium mix. Extruded bone china pellets. Photo Shannon Tofts.

It is the marks left behind when these materials burn out that are important. Traces can be deciphered, like a fossil turned to stone after millions of years, and the spaces they have occupied hold as much importance as the structure remaining. After firing, the work may be ground down or fiercely sandblasted, thereby wearing away even more than the fire has already consumed. Some surfaces look like a section of newly cut peat, rough and layered; some are ground or polished to a speckled surface resembling granite; sometimes a fine slipcast outer shell will show tension cracks where the thin exterior layer has shrunk more than the coarser clay body used for the interior; other pieces may have an inner granular surface formed by spraying a coating of metamorphic rock such as schist or slate taken from the site, then ground very fine.

Tony's experience as a designer means that he has no difficulty in planning, whether for one piece or for a series, and foreseeing all the stages ahead, from collecting and preparing the materials needed, to turning and casting large plaster moulds for specific pieces. The moulds may be used only a few times before being broken up, and since their life is seen to be limited, their use is not felt to be inhibiting. Sometimes only a section of a large shape will be used to create a different form. Working in a college gives access to a variety of equipment not usually available to a studio potter, and Tony is able to make use of grinding wheels, turning lathes and sandblasting machinery – more usually associated with glass or metalwork than pottery – to achieve a particular result.

Methods and Materials

Many pieces are vessel or bowl forms built within a plaster mould to a thickness of 3 to 5cm (1 to 2in). The crumbly clay body is compressed using a series of tools – from roofers' wooden shapes for moulding lead flashing via his father-in-law's drumsticks, to a final burnish with a rubber kidney – causing the body to pack and bind together until the required density is reached. Drying out needs to be slow to allow the moisture to evaporate evenly and avoid warping or distortion.

During bisque firing to 1200°C or 1250°C the work is supported in the kiln, and afterwards may be rubbed down with wet and dry, or further ground or filed to sharpen angles or define an edge. Oxides are then worked into the surfaces and may afterwards be partially rubbed away to leave colour only in the interstices, or several layers of stains may be built up to achieve the required degree of depth and intensity. Changes of colour often mark the interior/exterior with strong light and dark contrast. Bone china is strongly alkaline, and oxides such as vanadium react with it giving grey blues; copper sulphate is used for turquoise, and soluble salts such as iron chloride and potassium permanganate are absorbed gently into the surface, emphasizing edges and corners. The pieces may be fired and refired several times until the desired effect is achieved.

Structure and Landscape

POLLY MACPHERSON is interested in mixed media in many forms, not necessarily only ceramic, and is particularly keen on drawing and the drawings of other artists. In her own work she explores the underlying structure of the seemingly disparate elements found in nature, and the ways in which these can be organized to form a visual composition while still maintaining the identity of the original components. Unusually for a potter she places as much emphasis on drawings as on three-dimensional work, and feels that some of her ideas may be best expressed through drawing alone. The contrast between extremes is a driving interest, and is one of the reasons she adds other materials such as straw into her work – she describes this as 'playing with the eye'; A texture may *look* as though it is constructed from hay or straw, but in fact it has burned away, and the soft, natural material has turned to a hard, solid form.

Firing in a sawdust kiln seemed a natural progression from including combustible materials in the work itself. The forms need the subtle colouring from flame and flashing, and it allows the piece to be taken from the fire at any stage and re-oxidized if necessary. The uncertainty can be enjoyed and the options remain open.

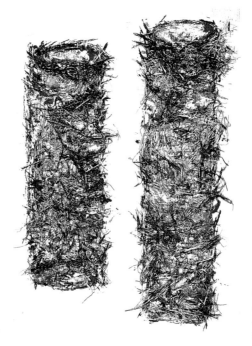

Tubes drawing by Polly Macpherson. Pastel, hay and paint.

Six tubes construction by Polly Macpherson, 1996. Earthenware slip with straw, sawdust-fired.

10 Mythical Beasts

Animals, real or imaginary, have long been part of an artist's repertoire, used as a metaphor to express strength, anger, ferocity, speed and beauty, as well as deep atavistic feelings now often buried in a modern world. Since a work is likely to express action or emotion, and making it is frequently done at speed while the mood is right, to be able to work without technical problems is a huge benefit. Maintaining freshness while working on a large piece without it becoming laboured or overworked has always been a problem, and many sculptors who enjoyed the spontaneity of clay but found the technical difficulties tedious, are turning to paperclay from other more conventional materials because of the freedom they feel that it gives to the way in which they can work.

They have found that using paperclay, or clays containing fibre additives, relieves them of many of the difficulties they faced before, in particular that of propping a heavy body on long, thin, potentially fragile legs, or of having to keep the whole structure damp enough for work to be continued on a large piece over a long period. Paperclay allows this expansion of scale because although a piece may be massive, it is still much lighter than it would be with

'Horse's Head' by Peter Hicks. Stoneware paperclay with copper oxide rubbed in; once-fired to 1260°C in electric kiln.

normal clay; moreover the amazing green strength of the material makes working on a large piece much more possible, even when it is not going to be moved. It also makes once-firing an option that is chosen by many potters: since the chance of kiln accidents is much reduced, the bisque firing can be omitted, saving time, energy and cost.

Paperclay is a rather lumpy material, and the presence of the fibre makes burnishing or creating a smooth surface difficult unless the body is first coated with a smoother slip.

The sculptures made with paperclay, therefore, tend to be built up leaving evidence of the modelling method, and with emphasis on texture. It is not really the best material for creating calm, smooth surfaces, or for carving soft, rounded forms. Much of the work made with it tends for that reason to be lively and energetic, with a feeling of movement only just held in check, and of action waiting to happen.

Making any sculptural piece, particularly on a large scale, demands an understanding of space, line, plane and surface qualities; it is also important to consider the work in relation to its surroundings and to the base which anchors it. These are challenges which even paperclay cannot solve on its own.

'Raven' by Peter Hicks, 1998. Crank paperclay with copper oxide applied when bone dry; once-fired in electric kiln to 1260°C. 30cm (12in) high.

Peter Hicks

Some years ago Peter Hicks, a long-time sculptor, took a ceramics course and discovered paperclay: he has used it ever since, finding that it is ideally suited to his style of work. Previously he had used wire armatures with a covering of resin mixtures, or shaped metal or plastics, but all these took longer to dry or to fashion, and he found that this precluded spontaneity so that he was never completely satisfied with the finished results. Peter is looking to evoke a sense of movement, trying to capture a fleeting moment or an action only caught from a brief glance. His recent work has featured birds of a variety of sizes and types, but all with a predatory, rapacious look – no tame domestic fowl here! These are birds of prey: wary, ready to take flight on the instant, with sharp beaks and spiky feathers – and the use of roughly modelled clay textures and features emphasized with thick oxides adds to the menacing effect of the evil owls or scavenging ravens that he depicts.

Methods and Materials

When starting an animal piece Peter often builds the legs first, stiffening them quickly by heating them with a paint stripper gun so that he can continue modelling without a pause. The hollow body can then be built up with soft clay, and paperclay slip used to seal joints, with an occasional blast from the gun to stiffen a part when necessary. Should any part of the work become too dry, it is just as easy to soak it and add new wet clay with slip.

Peter has used crank clay, grogged white stoneware and grogged red earthenware, all with equal success. His recipe uses a 50/50 mix of clay and paper, quite a high proportion, but probably acceptable because of the presence of grog in all the clays used. Grog does not change in the firing, and the particles support the structure of the clay when the cellulose burns away. Half a teaspoon of bleach is added to every bucket of the mix, and he finds this lasts for weeks without any moulds forming. The paper used is usually toilet tissue. The sculptures are finished with oxides, added at the dry stage and sponged off as necessary. Peter has found that he no longer needs to bisque fire, so the work is once-fired to maximum temperature – and he has never yet had a piece break in the kiln.

PROPPING

While certain pieces of large-scale work may still need an armature, the fact that paperclay shrinks less than clay means that the piece is less likely to crack as it dries. Internal supports for large pieces can be made from rolled cylinders of paperclay, or from a sort of scaffolding of stiffened paperclay strips; this will strengthen the work in progress, and it then becomes an integral part of the inside of the sculpture after it has been fired. Using this method means that the framework and the surface it is supporting dry and shrink at the same rate. External propping may still be necessary in the kiln during firing, for instance to prevent legs buckling or the piece slumping before the clay has matured sufficiently to bear the weight.

Ian Gregory

Ian Gregory, a long-time devotee of paperclay and an adventurer willing to try all sorts of methods, uses a range of materials for supports, including chicken wire, canes, metal rods – anything that will allow him to work at great speed on pieces that are full of energy and movement. If the piece is to be raku fired the metal support may even be left in place throughout the firing since the temperature will not be too great. Other materials will burn away. Some of his sculptures are

*'*Hound Dog*' by Ian Gregory. The dog has been built on a kiln shelf, and an 'instant' kiln constructed around it. The fibre blanket and layer of sand allow movement in the kiln during firing.*

'Hound Dogs K9' by Ian Gregory. Made on chicken wire armatures filled with bubble wrap. Equal mixture of 25 per cent pulp paperclay and earthenware, fired to 1100°C.

now so large that they have to be built *in situ*, and have their own individual kiln built around them.

Each piece seems to contain the essence of the animal or figure that he constructs, or the emotion that he is aiming to express. It is not necessarily a literal depiction, though all the figures are recognizable and can be understood: it is rather an interpretation of a particular facet from the inner nature of each one. Each can be enjoyed at a surface level, but each also contains other forces beneath: sometimes withdrawn and contemplative; sometimes benign and almost comic; sometimes threatening and holding more than a hint of menace; occasionally even triumphant and crowing with success.

Ian works quickly, and builds kilns almost as fast to suit whatever project is on hand. He may fire to raku temperature, then use the smoke effects from post-firing reduction to emphasize unglazed areas or to alter glaze qualities; at other times he may choose earthenware or stoneware temperatures; or he may even risk the dangers of salt glaze. This is an unforgiving medium, showing up every mark made on the surface of the piece, but it also gives a particular liveliness and quality which is quite unlike any other. The surfaces reflect the mood the piece is aiming to transmit. Rounded, meditative figures may be constructed from small dabs of clay that are built up to make the form, then paddled flatter to give a gently curving surface which seems smooth, but still retains the traces of how it was made. Larger areas of limbs or torso contrast with more smoothly modelled hands or heads. Cockerels are spiky, with quickly pulled detail and jagged edges, while the sleekness of the salt-glazed surface adds a suspicion of menace to the surface of some of the hound dogs. Pigs made from large sheets of clay roll and flop with a sleepy indolence.

The link between man and animals is also explored in his work, which frequently draws from myth and legend: grotesque, earth-bound figures with large heads like gargoyles may have small birds perched on their shoulders, or be launching fierce, rapacious-looking winged creatures off into space. Caliban and Ariel come to mind, the earthbound and the ethereal, or body and spirit.

Susan Halls

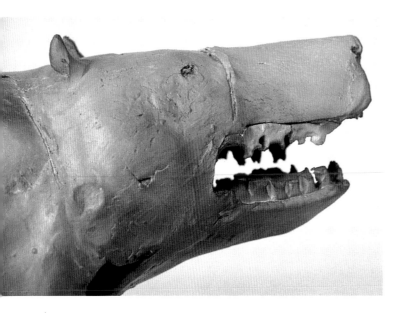

Susan Halls is another of the early expo-
nents of paperclay who has found that
the material allows her the freedom
to get on with what she wants to
make without worry. She discovered
it in 1990 during a residency in Banff,
Canada, and has used nothing else for
years – now she finds normal clays just too limiting. At that time
she was trying to enlarge the scale of her animal sculptures, but
found difficulties as the clays she was testing cracked, split and
flopped. Rosette Gault was working next door, and at her suggestion
Susan added paperpulp and chopped nylon fibre to her own mix of
clay slops. She describes the effect as instant and magical, producing a
material that was a combination of textile and cardboard – 'pliable
and chewy', to use her own words. A slab has length, width and
thickness; when rigid it is a building material, but when soft it
resembles a textile. She found that the material could be rolled
into large slabs, stretched, and draped like a skin, and that the textures created by these processes – with
wrinkles, stretch marks and a sort of
hairiness – were appropriate to the work
she wanted to make.

The basic recipe she developed then has
not really been changed since, and she
still adds chopped nylon fibres to the
clay mix. While in Banff her original
paper pulp was donated by a local factory,
but later on, back in Britain, she tried
newspaper and cardboard before settling
on mashed-up egg boxes or fruit trays. At
that time it was also difficult to obtain
chopped nylon or polyester fibres in this
country, so Susan tried hair from barber
shop sweepings. (It is interesting that in
exactly the same way, old-time builders
would add horsehair to the plaster mix
before plastering a wall: the hair acts as a
binder, making a mesh which holds the
other materials together.) In Susan's case,
while the hair worked well enough in the
raw clay, she felt uncomfortable using it,
and it made a dreadful smell when burning out in the firing; so it was a relief when
a manufacturer was found who was willing to supply chopped polyester.

*'Bad Dog .... rumoured Moose' by Susan Halls. This was her first
paperclay piece, made in 1991. Constructed from soft slabs of stoneware
paperclay including nylon fibres, raku fired with colloidal slips.
44 × 24 × 22cm (17 × 9 × 8in) (top).*

*'Growling Dog', detail, by Susan Halls, 1996. Method as described in
previous caption.*

Method and Materials

Susan's recipe is about 20 per cent paper pulp and 8 per cent (dry) polyester fibre added to a sloppy clay body, though sometimes she will add extra pulp if she wants the paper to have more effect. Recently she has tried out plant fibres from the seed pods of a plant (unknown to her) found near her present home in Connecticut, but these rot quickly and do not have much strength, only suiting small-scale work. The unfired strength is an important factor in Susan's work, as is the reduction in weight for murals and wall pieces. Different clays are used depending on the type of piece being made, and glazing and firing are carried out at all the usual temperatures, whether for raku, earthenware, stoneware or salt/soda.

Her early work was fierce, often featuring dogs, or heads of dogs, with fangs and gaping mouth – but at the same time with strangely human expressions. These were made from soft slabs of paperclay folded and bent into shape, coloured with colloidal slips and raku fired. A series of flying lemurs (believed in Roman mythology to be the spirits of the dead) and monkeys followed, growing lighter and almost airborne, their attitudes seemingly arrested in mid-leap; gradually these began to assume more and more human attributes until the figures became part animal, part human, or human figures were shown along with animals or birds, sometimes with the scale distorted. Recent work uses the female form in a softer, more voluptuous way, though still with a sharp wit and sense of humour.

Some work is now in the form of relief tiles or wall panels: these Susan makes by nailing a slab to the wall and working on it vertically, then 'ripping it off when leather-hard' as she describes it. She has now also started applying collaged paper on to the surface of her finished pieces, so that paper is an integral part of every stage. It is within the structure of the clay, used for post-firing smoking, and finally applied to the surface.

'Bird Tiles' by Susan Halls, 1999. Earthenware relief tiles with oxides, each approximately 15 × 15cm (6 × 6in).

Janet Hamer

Janet has become known for her well observed and meticulously modelled bird forms, enriched with lustrous glazes. Whilst each species is easily recognizable, they are more than merely realistic representations, and display the very characteristics of each bird, the lustre glaze echoing the gleam of light on feathers. The birds are hand built, and Janet has developed a method that she describes as 'slop casting', for which she uses two-piece plaster moulds to make the basis of some of the forms. The paperclay slop (made from porcelain and toilet tissue) is poured directly into the mould, and the plaster absorbs the surplus water; as the central pool sinks the mix can be coaxed up the sides to keep an equal thickness. When both halves of the mould are stiff, or even dry, they are joined, and details such as wing tips or feathers can be added or embellished. Fine points such as beaks and bills may be modelled in porcelain for greater smoothness and hardness, and coloured with stains.

'Gannets' by Janet Hamer. Porcelain paperclay with pure porcelain detail.

Contemporary ceramic sculptors who find their inspiration in animal form seem almost deliberately to be avoiding any suggestion of prettiness or the softness of a household pet in their work. It may be that the earthiness of the material makes for a bolder depiction, and the speed with which paperclay can be worked makes it more direct, but the elements exhibited in the work of all those illustrated here are primeval and strong: they show an instinct for survival, and there is no hint of sweetness.

Brendan Hesmondhalgh

Brendan does not use paperclay, but he does add cut polyester fibres to alter the handling characteristics of his clay, and so has been included here. His chosen clay is T-material, a strong white stoneware body containing grog in the form of molochite, which is much used by handbuilders and valued for its strength and forgiving nature. This clay already has high tolerances in terms of the length of time it can be worked on and have additions made to it, as well as surviving high firing temperatures. At other times a mix of craft crank and raku clay may be used. These clays are red in colour, incorporate a high proportion of fireclay grog and are generally coarser in texture. Raku clays are formulated for low temperature firing and the grog is to open the body and allow it to withstand the thermal shock of sudden heating and cooling. Crank can be fired to stoneware, at which temperature the impurities (usually iron) in the body will melt, and speckles will show on the surface of the piece.

The polyester fibre is chopped into approximately 3mm (⅛in) lengths, and wedged into the wet clay as it is mixed. The fibre will melt and burn away at quite a low temperature (280–300°) in the kiln; its purpose is to bind the raw clay, giving it more wet strength and flexibility for hand-building.

Brendan has always been interested in animals; he had various pets as a child, so his forms are created from memory as well as keen observation. He takes photographs and does many drawings before starting a piece, and makes sure to point out that he is not striving for an anatomical exactitude, but rather to portray an animal's specific characteristics of movement or form. He starts with screwed-up newspaper, which he fashions in roughly the shape of the head or body, or whatever part is being worked on; he then covers this with clay slabs which can be quickly wrapped and pressed to an approximation of the finished shape. At this stage the clay resembles a textile, behaving like a thick cloth which can be curved and folded and joined together easily, having almost the feeling of an animal hide. Texture is an important element in the work, and the gnarled wrinkles and marks that remain in the piece after drying and firing suggest not only the process of making, but also the tension and upheaval that have taken place in the life of the animal.

Once it is slightly stiffened the paper is withdrawn from inside, and the real modelling starts. The form may be stretched and pushed out from inside to suggest a curving belly or ribcage, or pressed in and elongated to delineate the tension of the muscle and bone. The various sections are selectively force-dried with an electric paint stripper until the legs are strong enough to support the torso, after which the head is added, and all the final detailed modelling and adjustments are made. Balance is another vital factor. Many animals look as though they are poised for flight, barely touching the ground and alert for signs of danger, yet every piece must have stability and be made to stand safely.

Firing takes place in an electric kiln: a bisque firing followed by stoneware to a top temperature of 1260°C. For the final firing the pieces may be treated with stains and oxides to highlight textures, and sometimes a very thin clear glaze is either sprayed or sponged on lightly to enrich particular areas. Other work may be further smoke fired in leaves or sawdust, with certain parts masked off for greater effect. Within the kiln some pieces may need careful propping to ensure that they do not collapse or the legs buckle. Legs are a major problem: the dogs, for example, are fired in saggars lying on their sides on a bed of silica sand with their legs carefully supported so that they do not bend. This means that only one or two pieces can fit into the kiln for each firing, and a careful support system has to be worked out for each one.

Like the other artists described in this chapter, Brendan is striving to portray the inner being of each animal he depicts, the particular attribute that makes it what it is. While he will often emphasize one special characteristic, he has no intention to over-simplify or to create a caricature, and there is certainly no hint in any of his work of anthropomorphic sentimentality.

'Pointer'
by Brendan
Hesmondhalgh.
Details as in previous
caption; smoke-fired.
87cm (34in) long
× 69cm (27in) high.

'Girls will be Girls'
by Susan Halls, 1998.
Modelled relief panel in
earthenware paperclay
with colloidal slips.
30 × 25 × 2cm
(12 × 10 × 0.8in).

Sometimes the boundaries between animal and human become blurred, with characteristics from both worlds fusing in surreal creations.

Gill Bliss

The work of Gill Bliss could certainly not be described as sentimental, though it might on occasion be considered caricature. In fact it is hard to know into what category it fits, like that of so many paperclay makers. Gill is a sculptor and model maker, and sometimes works as an animator; she likes paperclay for its directness, the speed with which it can be worked and fired, and the lack of problems generally encountered in constructing even complicated pieces. She, too, uses porcelain with toilet tissue. She feels that paperclay:

> … gives me a lot more freedom to create, without worrying whether things were too dry to join, or were of even thickness. In fact I can leave parts to become bone dry, giving a support to certain areas such as legs or wings, and then add on more clay to finish the figure.

Her figures are used in a similar way to animals in fables or folktales, to highlight human experiences. They have developed to include comment on contemporary social and political issues, but aim also to include humour and enjoyment in each piece. They are truly anthropomorphic, and sometimes it is hard to decide if they are animals with human characteristics or humans in disguise …

'*Pinstriped Frog*' by Gill Bliss. The frog is trying to conform with his clothing, but has to carry a mask to conceal his real self; in his other hand he carries a jewel, his secret inner self which is seldom revealed. Stoneware with paper pulp and coloured slips, fired to 1260°C. 30cm (12in) high.

'*Never Be Rude to Waiters*' by Craig Mitchell, 1992. Handbuilt earthenware with polyester fibre.
50 × 18 × 13cm
(20 × 7 × 5in).

11 Figures of Fantasy

Oval or pear-shaped figures, often small enough to be cradled in the palm of a hand, are amongst the earliest clay objects found in archaeological excavations all over the world. The figures are frequently female, thought to be votive offerings or fertility symbols, and may also have been used as amulets to ward off evil spirits. Both the human and animal forms have long been fashioned into clay figures linked to myth and magic and invested with religious or spiritual significance. That is still true today, and the elements of water, earth and fire are still strongly symbolic, although the meanings of the figures may be less apparent. Nevertheless, many artists feel that through the depiction of animal or human figures, deep-rooted atavistic fears or emotions can be expressed.

A three-dimensional piece carries weight, literally as well as figuratively. To view a figure from the back or side, to look down upon it, or into or through it, and to move from one angle to another almost seeing multiple views simultaneously, will give quite a different impression from that of a drawing or painting which must be considered only from a single plane. With a three-dimensional work the onlooker may also be able to touch the surface and to absorb through the fingertips the rough texture or smooth polish of a piece, and the contrast of one facet with another. This contributes to an understanding of the way in which the artist worked, whether with speed and intensity pressing pieces of clay together to capture a movement, or by a long, slow building up and burnishing to create an impression of solidity or calm.

In the past, many sculptors found that the vitality felt in working with such a tactile medium was outweighed by the many difficulties caused by working with clay over the length of time needed for the construction of a large piece. Problems included the difficulty of keeping the work moist enough, the distortion caused by pressure from too great a weight of clay, or the shrinkage of drying clay causing it to crack and pull away from an armature. To a large

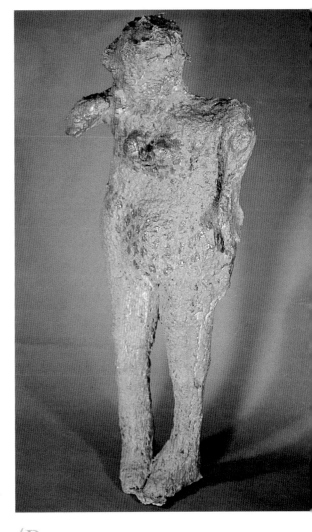

'*Baked Sunbather*' *by Lowell Baker, 1999. Wood fired, Cone 9. 56cm (22in) high. Photo Jackson A. Baker. This contemporary piece seems to have links with figures from a much earlier era.*

Bust by Roy Ashmore. Earthenware, cast in mould with straw and sawdust, parts later cut away to show interior structure.

extent paperclay has solved these problems, and now artists without previous experience of clay are choosing paperclay as a material because of its directness and the speed with which it can be worked. They come with knowledge of other materials, but without the craft-based discipline previously associated with clay, and bring new perceptions of what may be possible.

Because paperclay can be made and handled in large sheets, the basic structure can be assembled quickly. It is much lighter than normal clays, and can be used leather hard or almost dry, frequently supporting its own weight without the need for an armature; and since

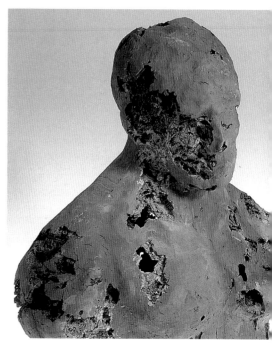

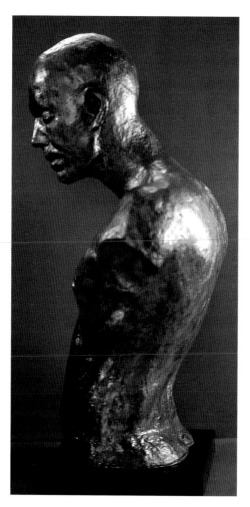

Torso by Ian Gregory. Sawdust, lentils and heavy grog crushed from HTI kiln brick. Salt glazed and post-reduction lustre, fired to Cone 10. 122 × 56cm (48in × 22in).

it shrinks less than normal clays, if an armature is needed, it is possible to leave it in position when the firing is to low temperatures, such as to those for raku.

Only the areas to be joined need to be damped, so that adding new clay becomes quite simple,. And wet clay or slurry can be layered over the surface at any stage to alter texture or strengthen joints. With much greater green strength, moving the work from bench to kiln is less hazardous, and the construction of pieces with spindly legs or outstretched arms is made possible. However, it must always be borne in mind that after firing the water will have evaporated, the organic loose additions burned away, and only the clay will be left, so the whole piece will be noticeably thinner and lighter. Thus a monumental piece should still possess enough weight to feel right,. There should be no chance of it blowing in the wind.

Employing a sort of belt-and-braces approach, clay for sculpture – and in particular for life-size or large pieces – is likely to contain both organic fibres and inclusions such as grog or molochite as additives. The interlocking tubular structure of the cellulose from the fibre acts as a binding agent, giving strength to the unfired clay, while the pre-fired grog particles help to hold the structure firm and prevent the body slumping in the heat of the kiln. The thickness of the clay will obviously be determined by the character and size of the piece, but as a rough guide it should be thick enough to allow the shape to be pushed out into curves from inside the slab, and to stretch considerably without cracking. Unlike most clays, it is not necessary for the walls of paperclay pieces to be of an exactly even thickness, and extra pads of clay can easily be pushed into the back of the slab to strengthen any weak points.

'Myself and Friend' by Janet Casson. Hand-built in white Vingerling clay; unfired.

Making Friends

JANET CASSON makes lifesize female figures, bird and fish-type forms, and is currently working on a totem pole that is comprised of casts from the faces of her friends. The enjoyment of observing people, and the idea of capturing thought or movement in clay, act as one creative spur, whilst architecture is another, particularly that of Gaudi with its convoluted curves and carving imitating the textures of trees, rocks and mountains. Janet builds her lifesize figures from the feet up, using a mixture of coils and slabs. Ideas 'just come', and will often change during the making, so that the finished piece may develop into something not envisaged at the start.

Method and Materials

Coiling is the method most used to construct the basis of the figure itself, with sheets of thinner clay forming drapery or coverings over this. Janet has found that it is an easy process to cut sections off and then reassemble them by sticking the parts together with slurry if the figure tilts, or if changes are felt to be necessary as it grows. Usually she will have more than one piece under construction at a time; each figure will take about a week for the initial making, though alterations may continue for some time – months even – till the whole feels right. Wet slurry may be added to the leather-hard surface to alter texture, and Janet has even covered a figure made from T-material with paperclay and refired it satisfactorily.

Janet lives in Norway, and her main problems are having a warm enough day for firing so that all the windows can be opened to clear the fumes when the fibre burns out, and waiting for the snow to melt so she can build a bigger kiln outside!

'Red Arm' by Lorraine Fernie, 1998. Porcelain paperclay with acrylic painting.

A Dreamer Dreaming Me

LORRAINE FERNIE comes from South Africa but now works in London, making sculptures based almost entirely on the female figure. Her previous work had a mystical, oriental feeling, sometimes using themes from legend and incorporating fish or other, part-imaginary creatures, all with a rather calm, contemplative quality. That work was often flat on one side, made to be wall-mounted like a strong relief, and the materials used were mostly unglazed T-material emphasized with oxides, with inclusions of coloured slip, and the use of cobalt blue and a copper glaze on certain areas.

Now, however, she has turned to paperclay, and her recent work has developed so that the figures – now always made to be seen in the round – twist and move in great sweeping curves as though arrested for a moment, and wait, poised to continue. Although some still stretch out languorously or pose reflectively, recent work has become less serene, and Lorraine describes it as a reaction to life – showing anger sometimes, or frustration or resignation. The figures often look inward, seeming engaged on some private contemplation. In Africa the bushmen believe that life is conjured from dreams, and that people or events materialize from the intensity of the mind's imaginings – and when asked 'but who makes you?' the response is 'a dreamer dreaming me'.

The figures are not large, but they appear bigger than they are, needing space around them. Forms are rounded, some limbs exaggerated, and curves are full and flowing, with heads and hands often small in scale and detailed. Colour is used for emphasis, softer tones wiped on in large brush strokes to delineate movement, or sharper detail picked out using strong colour or black.

'Homage to Louise Bourgeois' by Lorraine Fernie, 1998. Porcelain paperclay, cerulean blue acrylic paint allowed to run into lower part of figure, red acrylic lines to emphasize breaks from the division. 56cm long × 18cm high (22 × 7in).

Materials and Method

Lorraine explains that she starts construction by cutting slabs to size; these are then curved, and moulded from the inside before being joined together to form the shell of the figure. This allows adjustments to be made to modelling, pose and proportions before any 'filling' is added. The two halves of each figure are easily visible in a finished piece, and are used as a basis for a change of colour as well as a way of cutting the light that falls across the form clearly.

> I then carve away in any area where the forms are not clear enough. The method of construction should make this minimal, but pieces do also need to be added to in certain areas, and paperclay makes this much easier.

'Fleshpot – Stretching Figure' by Karen James. Earthenware fired to 1040°C. Coloured wax pastel applied when hot to soak into surface.

Once the proportions are established satisfactorily, layers of porcelain slip (without any paper content) are painted over the entire figure to build up texture and fine detail, and lines cut or scratched into forms as required. Sometimes at this point black stain is painted on, then partially rubbed off with a scourer.

Finally the figures are once-fired to 1260°C in an electric kiln. When cool, the surfaces are sanded with a graphite stick and then smoothed with a flexible diamond pad of the type used for polishing marble. The colours currently used are acrylic and are strong and punchy – a limited palette used with discretion in a painterly way to suggest covering, rather than copy, clothing. The acrylic is finally covered with a thin coat of matt varnish.

Start from the Heart

KAREN JAMES calls her figures 'Fleshpots' and always refers to them as 'ladies'. From a photograph they look as though they might be on a grand scale, but in fact although the curves are generous, the pieces are quite small and seem to ask to be handled. There is a warmth about them, but also a monumental quality which suggests the possibility of creating them on a larger scale. Karen comes from

America and now lives in Scotland where she finds the cold climate a real disincentive to physical activity – in spite of the current fashionable emphasis on fitness and creating the body beautiful. She remembers the effort it took to maintain a disciplined regime, and says:

> My ladies represent the easing of regime, abandon, and the uninhibited comfort one should have in one's own skin, as well as the acceptance of one's own self. The work needs the viewer's reaction to complete it. Most often this is amusement and recognition.

The response comes in reaction to the posture, rather than to fine details such as features or hair, and Karen finds the paperclay has a flesh-like quality both in forming and finishing that is lacking in conventional clay.

Methods and Materials

The material used is a mix of equal parts red clay, crank clay, and commercial paper fibre. Small pieces start as enclosed pinch pots, paddled into the shape of a heart which seems to give them life immediately. Larger pieces are coiled. Steel wool is used to smooth and refine the surface, and soft hair-like fibres appear. Pastel-coloured slips are applied to pieces which will later be treated with coloured wax, and oxides are used to enhance folds and recesses. At this stage steel wool is again used to remove excess colour.

'Fleshpot – Reclining Figure' by Karen James (above). Details as previous caption.

'Fleshpot' by Karen James. Detail of surface quality, made with coloured waxes on the piece when still very warm from the kiln.

Firing is to between 1000°C and 1040°C in an electric kiln, and the work is removed when it is still warm and treated with vivid wax or oil pastel colours. The paperclay draws oxides further into the body, and the burned-out fibre leaves a porous surface which holds the wax better than normal clay. The warm surface soaks up the colours and holds them with great intensity even when the piece has cooled. Final burnishing is done by buffing with a soft hairbrush. Some more natural pieces have grog added for surface texture and are fired to the higher temperature of 1120°C, then treated in the same way, but using a neutral wax. The result is a succulent surface with a luscious quality almost resembling ripe fruit.

'The Narcissus Fitness Technique' by Craig Mitchell, 1998. Hand-built earthenware with mild steel, brass and mirror. 30 × 30 × 10cm (12 × 12 × 4in).

Caught in the Act

The previous artists work on the whole piece from the beginning, seeing it as a single entity but allowing for change as the figure grows organically. **CRAIG MITCHELL** has a different approach: he meticulously designs his compositions in individual sections and makes templates before he starts, so that every detail of the animated composition has been well planned in advance.

'Poseidon and His Sports Walkman' by Craig Mitchell, 1998. Hand-built earthenware with nylon fibres. 90 × 48 × 40cm (35 × 19 × 16in).

Thoroughly Modern Mother' by Craig Mitchell, 1998. Earthenware and mild steel. 47 × 50 × 23cm (18.5 × 20 × 9in).

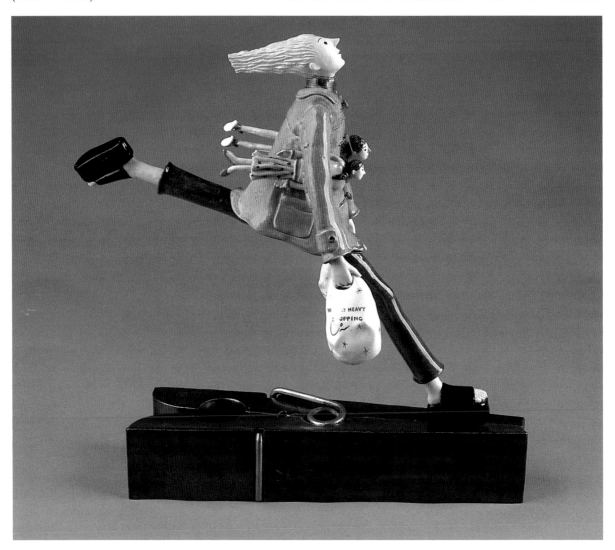

The figures are incredible, a fusion of old and new, mythical creatures and contemporary characters, their titles giving some clue as to their origins and the idea behind them. Lively, acrobatic, brightly coloured and usually provoking a smile, they look like a circus caught in an instant and turned, if not to stone, then to something that has arrested their flying movement for ever. If you look away for just an instant you expect them to have changed to an even more exaggerated position while your back was turned.

Methods and Materials

The figures are constructed from pieces cut out using templates rather like dress patterns – and in fact dress patterns shrunk to a small size on the photocopier have occasionally been used. Each segment is made separately and dried until it is stiff enough to be joined, then the various components are put together to form structurally safe sections. Much of the work is put together after firing, so the areas to be joined are roughened and left unglazed.

Craig uses Potclays grogged white earthenware which is bought in a plastic state then dried out, broken up, and slaked down to form slip. The grog in the clay body is necessary to strengthen the clay and stop it slumping in the kiln. Nylon fibre chopped very small is added to the slip: a handful to a bucket of slip seems to be a good measure, equating to 20g (¾oz) dry fibre to one 25kg (55lb) bag of clay, made into slip. The purpose of the nylon fibre is to increase the green strength, thus improving the handling properties of the body before it is fired: it melts at a comparatively low temperature in the kiln, fusing into the body, and does not ultimately add to the finished strength of the fired clay. The slip is thoroughly mixed in a blunger, then dried to a usable state, wedged and rolled very thin.

All the components are individually hand built, though the possibility of slip-casting some of the elements is being considered for the future.

After the first firing – which is hotter than the glaze one and is taken to 1180°C – the figures are carefully painted using commercial brush-on glazes. Since the spaces to be covered are often small and intricate, these glazes have been found to be the most suitable for the job. It is a time-consuming process, with adjoining areas masked off to avoid blurring, and multiple colours applied to every piece. The second firing is considerably lower than the first, reaching around 1000°C. Complicated figures are then carefully assembled, section by section, one part balancing another until the group is complete. Sometimes steel pins are inserted inside the body and then into a base to balance the piece, and other materials such as steel wire or wood may be added to complete the effect.

Fragile Shell

SARA CHALLONER'S two main concerns are childhood and armour, and at first sight they would not appear to have much in common. However, their link is vulnerability, and she uses clay to reflect protection in its relationship to the human figure. The child is a metaphor for anything in need of protection. The armour is the remnant left behind, the empty shell, and Sara has made it to look like children's clothing, through which the viewer is invited to imagine the vanished presence of the child. Many of the figures, or the parts of them that remain, have their arms upraised as though asking to be picked up. The material chosen to do this needed to be strong, so as to be able to withstand a rigorous making process, and at the same time fragile, to retain the feeling of vulnerability, and paperclay was the medium found to have both these opposite qualities. The work may have been fired several times – with all the attendant risks of breakages from fire or handling – but the finished piece appears hard, with a surface echoing burnished metal.

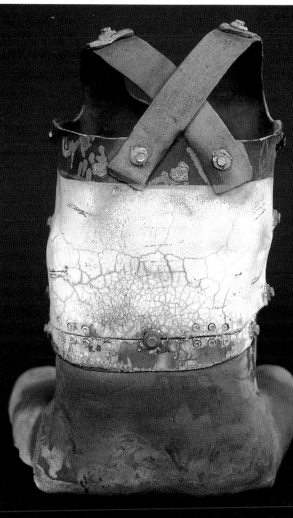

'Armour' by Sara Challinor. Front and back. The work is bisque fired to 1000°C in an electric kiln, glazed and fired again to the same temperature. Raku glaze is then sprayed on, and the figures refired very rapidly to 800°C, placed in a smoke bin and highly reduced.

Method and Materials

St Thomas' clay is dried out, then made into a slip with the addition of 30 per cent paper pulp. This is dried out and rolled into thin sheets and cut out, also using templates similar to a dress pattern. Each piece is then dried in a sort of hammock and stiffened with a paint stripper till leather hard. Sara says: 'You know they are drying when the steam has the distinctive smell of paperclay.' The sections are then assembled and joined by scoring and slipping with details such as rivets or bolts added, and fired to 1000°C in an electric kiln.

A white crackle glaze is used on some pieces, and they are fired again to a similar temperature. This is to give a shiny surface on which enamel can be printed before a further raku firing. Another copper matt raku glaze may also be sprayed on to certain areas, while others are masked off before this firing. Each piece is raku fired separately. The firing is taken rapidly to 800°C, then the work is removed and placed in a bin of sawdust in order to become highly reduced.

A Suggestion of Form

ROSALIND SIMPSON is another sculptor who has turned to ceramics and whose work is influenced by the human form. She, too, mentions armour, though in her case the torso has disappeared and is merely suggested by strap-like bindings wound around a hollow space. At first these were built over a former made from card or

'Bed of Roses' by Rosalind Simpson. White earthenware paperclay with tin glaze and copper lines.

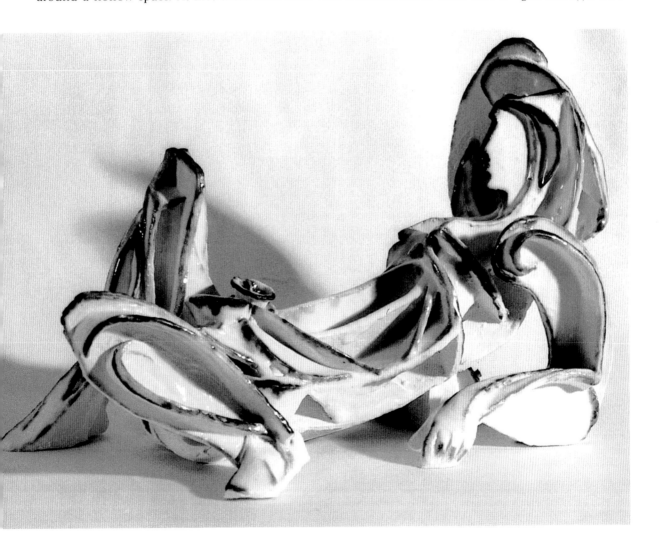

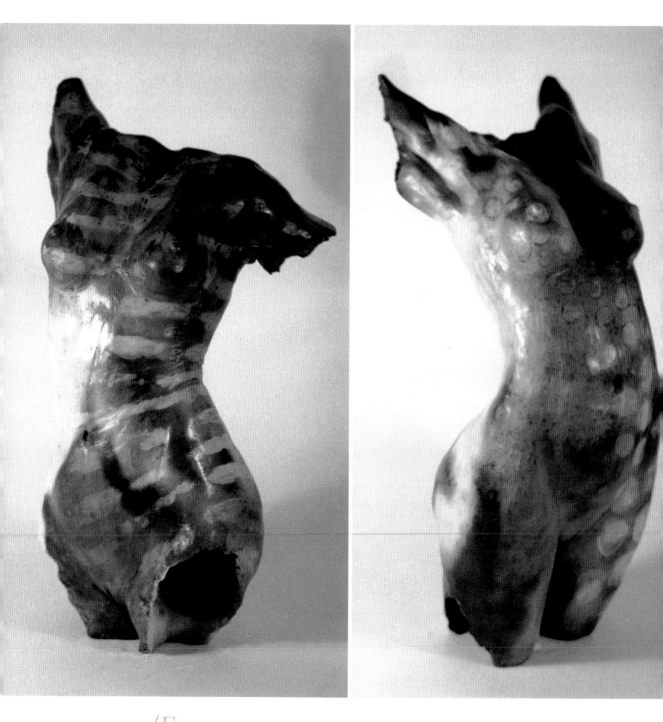

*'F*emale Form' by Gill Bliss. These figures aim to portray a sense of womanhood rather than individual characteristics. Bisque fired to 1100°C, then smoke fired in a bin of wood chippings. Patterns are made by painting the bisqued pieces with stripes or spots of clay slip which resist the smoke and are washed away after smoking, leaving a lighter colour. Waxed finish. 51cm (20in) high.

paper, but the shapes tended to collapse in the kiln when the support burned away, so now the straps are constructed to be self-supporting and are carefully joined where they cross or overlap. The material used is white earthenware, and this is covered with a white tin glaze with copper used for outlining edges, giving the effect of a three-dimensional drawing.

It appears that the female figure is very often the source of ideas, inspiration, or whatever name is given to the motivation for making a work. The interpretation may be idealized and ephemeral, as in the two smoked figures by Gill Bliss, graceful as fleeting shadows, it may be humourous but kindly, observing idiosyncrasies, as in the group that Susan Halls calls 'Accessories'; or it may be frankly cheeky and cocking a snook, as Ian Gregory's 'Lautrec Tart' – but all display lively, varied aspects of the female half of humanity. In contrast, Helen Smith takes a more enigmatic view in the piece she calls 'Wise Men'. The three figures are hooded, bound and ambiguous – indeed, they scarcely look human, although there are disturbing resemblances to images of the Klu Klux Klan. It is certainly not possible to know what they are thinking.

'Figures from the 'Accessories' series by Susan Halls, 1999. Pressmoulded and pinched earthenware with paper collage surfaces, each approximately 19 × 12 × 12cm (7 × 5 × 5in).

'Lautrec Tart' by Ian Gregory. Fifteen per cent paper pulp, crushed firebrick and HTI brick and sawdust. Raku fired with post-firing reduction. 91 × 23cm (36 × 9in).

'Wise Men' by Helen Smith, 1996. Bisque fired porcelain paperclay with copper wire, lightly smoked. Mounted on brass pillars with base made from T-material.

12 Vessels: the Space Within

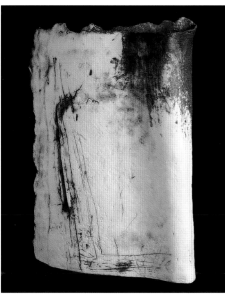

Many materials are used to make containers, but it is because clay is so versatile that it is a satisfying medium for a whole range of vessels. For many makers, vessels are the starting point for conceptual ideas, and the limitations of working within such a configuration are not seen as a constraint, but rather as a central discipline in the work. Often the domestic scale also feels a comfortable one in which to work.

Aside from its functional purpose of storage, a vessel can embody two other, very different ideas: either that of containment, concealment and secrets tucked away; or its opposite, an open dish or chalice such as might be used for an offering or libation. **AAGE BIRCK** likes the middle ground between 'art' and 'craft' that his container forms inhabit, and he adds found objects such as metal handles, knobs or locks to his pieces to emphasize their ambiguity.

Perhaps because it is simplest to make paperclay in sheets or slabs, there do not seem to be many potters using the traditional method of coiling to build vessels, and even fewer who find the material suitable for throwing. Coils can be manipulated in any direction, making them more fluid than slabs which tend to retain a certain rigidity; however, they can also be rather soft and floppy in the beginning stages, and need some sort of support until the base dries stiff enough to bear the weight of clay without distortion. It requires control to maintain the shape as the piece is built up stage by stage. Hollow

Two sides of the same vessel by Carol Farrow, one of the original developers of paperclay. Carol has continued to work both with handmade paper and with clay. Here the paperclay slab has been incised and pressed on to fabric before assembling, the surface mark-making considered in a similar way to a drawing. 1998. Photo Stephen Harper.

forms in paperclay are made most frequently by slab building or by using moulds.

For handbuilding, clay should be flexible enough to resist cracking over what may be an extended working period; it should be strong enough to hold the shape and resist warping; and finally it needs to be sticky enough to stay together, but does not have to be as plastic as clay used for throwing. Individual pieces must be designed keeping the making process in mind, and have a structural strength which does not over-extend the body with thin or unsupported areas. A sphere has great physical strength, and round pots were made long before wheel-thrown ware was common, though it may not necessarily be the best shape for paperclay. Paperclay fulfils most of these criteria, and is also tolerant of forced drying that enables work to continue more rapidly.

When making a vessel, the thickness of the wall is an important factor in relation to the interior space it encloses, and the relation of the volume contained by the inside wall must be considered in proportion to the outer surface and to the base. Rims and edges also define the shape, marking the change from outside to the interior, and their thickness, or thinness if they taper away, is an important factor. The size of the aperture in relation to the whole is another, determining the nature of the vessel and whether it aims to conceal secret spaces, or is open like a cup or a bowl.

Tall vessel form by Lizzie Rice. Porcelain paperclay, hand-built, barium glaze and slip decoration. 60 × 24cm (24 × 9in).

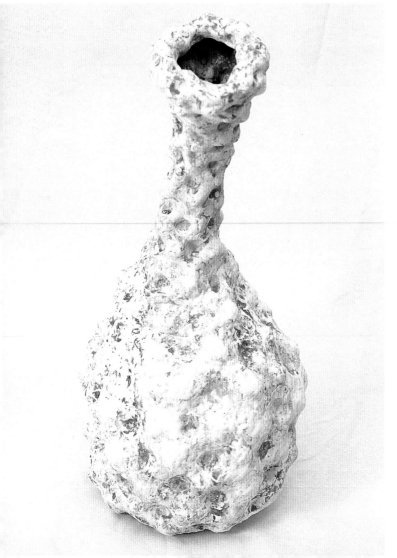

Secrets Within

LIZZIE RICE has developed her own technique. She came to use paperclay because the white clay that in fact she preferred would not have been tolerant enough on its own, and she needed a strong clay for hand-building. Her interests are in organic structures such as rocks, fungi and shells, and she wants to imbue her work with a feeling of movement and life. The surface is important, and the movement is carried around the whole piece, creating an undulating tension. The fact of the object being hollow is also important, the opening to the inside becoming like an eye, or a tunnel leading to the hidden and secret interior.

Method and Materials

To make her forms, Lizzie uses palm-sized pats of paperclay which are pressed together, each layer being dried out a little with a blow-torch before the walls are built any higher: this allows her to work quickly and spontaneously – and the paperclay is able to accept the pushing and pulling required to create the desired surface movement. Her preferred materials are a blend of two parts of David Leach porcelain mixed with one part of computer paper pulp for the body, though she has also tried white stoneware and red earthenware and other papers. The vessels are fired to earthenware temperature using barium glazes, with porcelain sip used to create the dappled textures.

Vessels Great and Small

PAUL BRADLEY lives on an island in Finland, a country renowned for papermaking. He came to paperclay because as a slab builder he realized he could cast slabs as large as he wanted, restricted only by the size of the casting surface, with much less difficulty than rolling and joining slabs in the conventional way. Transport is a major cost of island life, so his clay is delivered in powdered form; and the fact that adding paper makes the clay go further and his sculptural pieces weigh lighter, are additional factors in favour of paperclay.

Pear-shaped vessel by Lizzie Rice. Materials as in the previous caption. 40 × 36cm (16 × 14in).

Methods and Materials

For the paper content in his mix Paul uses newsprint, which he gets from a local printer; it comes from the unused ends of the huge rolls on which newspapers are printed. Paul says: 'When a roll is almost finished it would be too much work to rethread it, and though in many areas all these might be collected and recycled, here there is no one to do it, so I get them for free.'

The paper is torn into small pieces and blunged for several hours until the whole is like a thick porridge. From time to time the paper must be cleared from the blades of the blunger, and any wads that have collected broken up. When it has reached an even consistency the pulp is drained, and squeezed out by the handful to get rid of as much water as possible before being added to a previously prepared slip. Measuring is by eye and by feel alone – it must feel right. Paul describes this as '… adding paper pulp till the slip is so thick it will not mix effectively in the blunger, possibly about one cricket ball-sized handful of pulp to two litres of slip'.

It sounds like quite a high proportion of paper to slip, and may account for one problem which Paul has had: that of tall pieces slumping in the kiln at high temperatures,

'*Torsion' by Paul Bradley. Slab-built.*

damaging not only themselves but also falling on and sticking to others in the kiln. He solves this by building a structure of ribs within a piece to support it, and finds that the joining powers of paperclay make this quite a simple procedure. Paul's vessels range in size from 7.6cm (3in) to 90cm (3ft), so some are on a large scale.

Paul's experiences do highlight one of the lessons that has to be learned when using paperclay: namely that however firm and thick the material feels in the raw state whilst in the making, a great deal will burn away in the firing, and the finished piece will be much thinner. It will also have pores where the cellulose fibres once were, which makes it slightly porous even at high temperatures. Thus unfired paperclay can feel stronger than fired, particularly when the clay is very thin or has been high fired.

Containing the Light

The work of **ANGELA MELLOR** is of very different character since she is aiming at lightness and translucency, and her pieces are slip-cast in fine bone china with inserts of paperclay to add texture and a greater density.

Although she was born and educated in England, Angela has lived in Australia for some years and her work is redolent of light and the graceful flowing forms seen on a coral reef or in tropical foliage. Individual pieces are quite small, and they are often shown in a series, or in a related group of similar forms. Angela turns plaster on a lathe to make moulds, and, interested in natural growth, sometimes makes clay impressions of organic forms such as coral or shells which are also made into small moulds. Slip is poured into these, and when stiffened sufficiently they are applied as sprig decoration, or as feet or handles to a piece. One series used the shape of the datura flower as an

Coral bowl by Angela Mellor, 1997. Bone china with paperclay inset. 9.5cm (3.7in) diameter.

inspiration; in another, photographs of the shadows of leaves gave ideas for the decoration; and yet another combined deep blue *pate de verre* glass in flowing wave forms with delicately balanced translucent white cups. The pieces have great delicacy, but at the same time are clear and strong, open to the light.

Casket by Suzhanna Perryman. Forms built up by soaking scrim and muslin in porcelain and red earthenware slip, interior glazed with high alkaline glaze. 30cm (12in) high.

Methods and Materials

Torn strips of paperclay are applied inside the mould before the bone china casting slip is poured in, so that the paperclay becomes an integral part of the vessel, accentuating the varying degrees of translucency. The cast can be made even finer by painting a design in shellac on the dry surface of the bone china after it has been taken from the mould, then sponging away gently. The shellac acts as a resist, so the coated areas remain thicker and give the effect of shadows when the light shines through. Colour may be added using water-soluble colorants (mainly chlorides), which add to the luminosity when the piece is lit from above. Bone china is taken to a higher temperature in the bisque than the glaze firing, and work is supported in setters at this stage.

The Light Flows Through

SUZHANNA PERRYMAN is also striving for lightness in pieces that look fragile but are actually quite strong. Her work is in the form of closed containers, inspired by caskets and reliquaries once intended to house sacred relics, but now retaining only the memory of such an event. She says: 'The emptiness of the hollow forms is symbolic of the mysticism that has receded from our daily lives. The closed pieces reflect a desire to preserve a declining spiritual aspect.' The flow of air, light, and symbolically spirit, is an important factor in considering each piece.

Methods and Materials

The methods for making show very clearly in the finished work. Different fabrics – gauze, muslin, hessian and tapestry canvas – are soaked in red earthenware or porcelain slip, and wrapped around formers made from combustibles such as paper, card or sticks. The materials are loosely woven, and must be made from natural, rather than man-made fibres – for example scrim, or the fine mesh muslin used for bookbinding – because these absorb the slip; they also give an open structure to the fired object. After bisque firing the forms are spray glazed on the inside, sometimes with the addition of copper to give turquoise, resulting in a strongly textured, organic surface. Forms are enclosed one within another, coarser fabrics outside and finer ones used for inner layers, but leaving windows or spaces to give a glimpse through to the hidden inner containers.

A Contrast of Opposites

FRED GATLEY's work is not about pots in any traditional sense. It cuts across many boundaries, encompassing skills from numerous disciplines – engineer, metal worker, potter, silversmith and glass polisher – all meticulously studied and applied, although he believes that of the ceramist is to the fore. The finished pieces are deceptively simple to look at – like eggs from a magical vanished bird – with a strongly speckled body and smooth polished surface, gleaming like a hard wet stone. Each piece is small scale and finely detailed, demanding close examination, and the differing surfaces yearn to be touched. When handled, the bowls have the quality of polished marble or granite.

The ceramic forms rest on cast metal bases, each one different and made specifically for the bowl which it will support; they are heavily textured and patinated, and are also raised on gold or silver feet to lift them both physically and visually. The bowls are

Inner casket of the previous piece by Suzhanna Perryman.

often supported on pinnacles enhanced with silver or gold. The aim is to produce pieces of work with a balanced contrast. Each bowl is simply presented, almost offered up, on a base which opposes it in every way – in shape, colour, weight, feel and material: with the texture of rough stone or petrified lava, it provides the strongest possible contrast to the smoothness of the polished clay. The intention is that the two are such opposites that they both complement and enhance each other. The result is highly sophisticated, an offering small in scale but precious as a jewel, deserving contemplation.

Methods and Materials

Fred's methods have been developed and perfected over a long time, and have involved much trial and error. He started off by incorporating copper filings into porcelain, pinching this into small pots fired to 900°C; at this stage he could wet and dry these to a reasonably fine finish. When the temperature was taken higher (to 1220°C), however, he ran into trouble, because the copper melted within the clay body and erupted through the walls of the piece like volcanic warts or blisters. Inclusions of other metals were similarly unsatisfactory, needing large amounts of work after firing to get even close to the sort of finish he desired. It was at this point that he came up with the idea of making low-fired, coloured grogs which could be easily crushed and added to the body, with the metals used separately for the bases.

*P*orcelain bowl with copper inclusions on bronze and steel base with brass feet.

*B*lack-stained bowl with large grog inclusions on steel base by Fred Gatley. Bowl 6cm (2.4in) diameter.

The bowls are made in moulds by a jollying process; this gives a uniformity which makes the final polishing simpler. Using conventional glass polishing methods for the outside, and specially made polishing domes for the interiors, a gleaming final finish can be achieved; most pieces are completed with renaissance wax.

13 Moulds, Formers and Armatures

Even with a material as strong and adaptable as paperclay, there are times when some support is necessary due to the size and weight of the piece, or because it has a shape which could not be achieved by any other means. Moulds roughly divide into two types: hump or hollow.

Hump Moulds

A hump is the simplest type of mould, and is exactly what the name implies: a one-piece shape over which the clay is draped. The upper surface of the clay when it is placed on the mould therefore becomes the underneath of the finished piece once it is lifted off, and this is useful in allowing a foot-ring or base to be attached while the clay is still well supported on the mould. While a shallow curve will allow the clay to shrink and rise away from the mould, care must be taken not to leave a tighter piece on too long, or even paperclay may shrink sufficiently to crack.

Moulds and materials by Polly Macpherson, 1995. Forms and textures built on a circular former.

A small piece of clay pressed over a large mould will give a very shallow shape that may fall back even more in the kiln, so it is as well to define the form clearly and to emphasize it more than may seem necessary in the raw state. Conversely, a large slab of clay can be draped over a small mould to give a fluid, pleated or gathered effect. Almost anything can be used as a hump mould provided it has a surface that the clay will not adhere to: boulders, balls, blocks of polystyrene – even plastic bowls, buckets and drainpipes can be used if they are first wrapped with strips of newspaper. The slightly wrinkled texture this gives to the inside of the object can be used to good effect, or can later be smoothed away.

Bisque Formers

For a longer lasting, but still simple solution my own preference is for bisqued clay shapes, which I have found to be lighter and much harder wearing than the plaster more commonly in use. The ones I have been using for many years are merely simple thrown bowls in a variety of sizes, their outside surface originally burnished to a smooth shine, and now with an additional patina developed through use. More complex shapes might not be so easy. Mine are used as humps because I want the interior of the bowl to be smooth (and some favourite shapes have made more than 600 bowls!), but if you are a thrower it is just as easy to make a bowl, then either smooth out throwing rings with a rubber kidney, or deliberately make an interesting surface inside the form that will then texture the outside of a piece pressed within it. A catenary curve is strong, and bowls made with that contour hold their shape well without slumping or warping. Sometimes only part of a large mould may be used to make a curved section for a joined piece.

A selection of thrown formers made from porcelain finely turned and burnished, then fired to 1150°C and further smoothed with wet and dry. This makes them hard-wearing but still porous. Plaster hump moulds sometimes absorb moisture so quickly that the clay is almost sucked onto the surface, and pieces made from thin clay can be hard to remove. These were made in 1985, and hundreds of pieces have been made from each one. The largest is 43cm (17in) in diameter.

Moulding in Sand

For large-scale work a sand mould is fairly quickly constructed from a heap of fine damp sand pressed and paddled into the desired shape. The clay can be pressed directly onto this, in which case the finished surface will have a grainy texture; the actual sand stuck to the clay mostly brushes off as the clay dries. Alternatively, a cloth or thin sheet of plastic can be stretched over the sand, helping to firm the moulded shape and make it last for one or two more usages; this makes the inside of the piece rather smoother, the cloth or plastic being peeled off from the inside of the piece once it has been lifted from the sand. Moulds like this can be made on a large bat on the wheel if a round bowl or dish is wanted, but they really come into their own for curving forms or spirals which can be sculpted very freely and would be much more difficult done in any other way.

A bag of sand – or sawdust, or even polystyrene chips if they are small enough and the bag is strong enough to hold them tightly together – can be pushed into any shape, and can also make a firm, curving hollow like a pillow to support a rounded base or rounded sections as they are joined. A more tubular bag can be used inside a tall, thin form as a support till it is firm enough to stand alone; before firing the bag can be untied and the sand poured out to use again, provided an aperture is left. The empty bag can either burn out inside the form, or be pulled out if there is space enough.

Sand in a box – like a child's sandpit – can just as easily be sculpted into hollow shapes, lined with a cloth and the clay sheet laid in until it is stiff enough. The box – or a cottle, like that used for a plaster mould – is needed to keep the shape firm, otherwise the pressure when the clay is pushed in causes the hollow to collapse. The sand must always be fine, and damp enough to be paddled firmly, otherwise it will not retain the shape.

It is quite simple to make a quick plaster mould in a sand hollow too, by modelling out the shape in reverse in the sand – taking care not to get undercuts – then gently pouring in plaster; when it is removed from the sand it will (of course) be a hump mould with a grainy surface. This is rather a crude method, but good for something like a series of masks since the clay will be laid over the plaster and the sandy surface will therefore be inside the mask and unseen. It is also easy to make several casts from the original model, changing each one slightly to alter mood or expression.

Other Supports

All sorts of materials are used for interior supports – crumpled newspaper, blown up balloons, polystyrene beads, cardboard tubes – depending on the size and shape of the work. Newspaper and cardboard are fine if the piece is light or can be stiffened quickly with a heat gun for example, but they rapidly absorb the damp from the clay and may become too soft to give much support otherwise. However, they can be left to burn out within a closed form without real problems so long as the form is strong enough to support itself without sagging. The card will burn out well before the clay is hardened.

Blown up balloons are not very strong, but may help a fine piece to retain its shape for long enough to stiffen. They can be inserted into quite a narrow aperture and then

Earthenware forms before firing by Suzhanna Perryman. Hessian is soaked in slip and rolled round cardboard tubes which burn out in the kiln.

inflated if a fragile piece shows signs of collapse, and pierced with a pin through the wall of the pot to release the air before firing if they haven't already gradually deflated of their own accord. Polystyrene beads in a bag act in a similar way to sand, but should be poured out before firing as they give off noxious fumes when burned.

The same forms bisqued, waiting to be glazed on the interior.

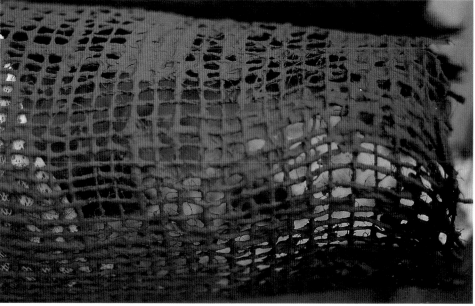

Armatures

An armature is the name given to a structure usually placed inside a form, which supports it during the making process. Armatures are most used by sculptors, and if clay was the medium being used for modelling it had to be kept damp to prevent it shrinking and cracking away from the support (that is, until paperclay). This entailed much tedious wrapping and spraying, when work was drawn out on a large or complex piece. The finished work was then cast in plaster and the mould used for further casts, either in plaster or other materials. The original model was never fired.

'Waste Armatures' devised by Frank Smith. The paperclay covers the armature made from waste polystyrene and can be seen just beginning to shrink away from the lower edge.

Frank's 'One Offs'

Whilst looking for a simple way of producing complex shapes in ceramic similar to those carved in wood or stone, **FRANK SMITH** drew on his knowledge of industrial casting techniques. In this a variety of materials may be used to make the pattern, the cheaper ones for shapes only wanted once. These – such as wax for the process known as 'lost wax' casting – are burnt out by the heat of molten metal during the casting process, leaving little or no residue.

Frank decided to try a combination of paperclay and polystyrene. The polystyrene came from the packing round large electrical items, which dealers are generally delighted to get rid of at no charge. Sometimes this is already in complex shapes suggesting further forms, or thicker blocks can·be made by gluing sheets together. These are shaped with a variety of tools – surform, hacksaw, rasp, file or sandpaper – until the final shape has evolved. The surface is not important as it will be inside the finished piece, which will be larger than the armature by the thickness of the clay used to cover it.

During this testing period, Frank designed deliberately complex forms with many joins to test the material in all directions, and few problems with cracking were found, even when dry pieces were added later. Sections of clay can be cut

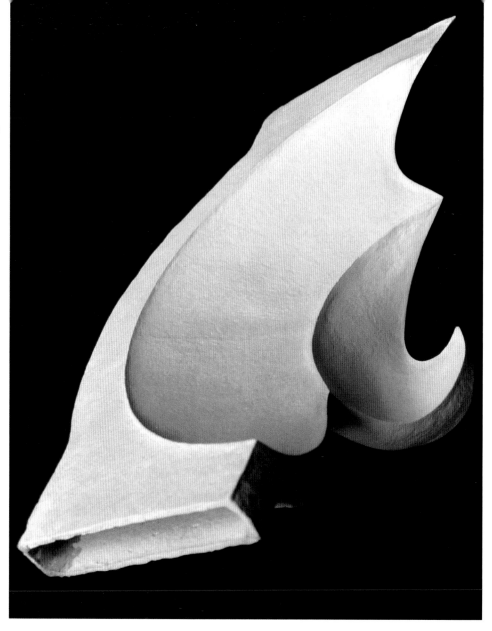

A *similar piece after firing. The polystyrene has burned away in the kiln and the piece is now hollow.*

roughly to shape with scissors, then pressed very firmly together over the armature, using more force than is possible with a hollow form. The clay is used quite damp, as this is most flexible and easily manipulated, and slurry is trowelled onto joints before fitting them together. Any cracks which do appear during drying are repaired with slurry.

As the clay dries it compresses the polystyrene so that it bulges out from the base of the work. This makes it unstable and likely to topple in the kiln, particularly when there is a release of gas during the firing, so the work is bisque fired on its side with nothing blocking the base openings. Polystyrene gives off unpleasant fumes so it is important that the kiln area is well ventilated.

The clay used is a smooth white stoneware mixed in approximately 75:25 ratio with pulp from old photocopying paper, and to date firings have been to earthenware temperatures with oxides and an alumina glaze to finish.

Large-Scale Spraying

LOWELL BAKER is a college lecturer in America, and he is always searching for new techniques to enable his students to develop their ideas further. The addition of cellulose fibres was originally used to make quick saggars to contain more fragile forms for firing, but the saggars often turned out to be more interesting than the pieces they contained, and the idea of blowing or spraying paperclay onto large forms was born. The type of sprayer sold in builders' merchants to spray textured paint or stucco was found to be a relatively low-cost tool which did the job effectively, but a non-pressurized sandblaster (the sort sold in car supply stores) is also good if thin coats of slip are to be applied.

The form is usually made from blocks of foam cut and glued together, and shaped with a knife or scissors or cut on a bandsaw. This is placed on a sheet of polythene so that any overspill of slip can be retrieved and reused, and spraying is usually done out of doors. Very large work can be suspended within a frame to help keep it upright and support the weight as successive coats of slip are applied. If this method is used, a layer of slip should be spread over the bottom, or a thin sheet of plastic clay put underneath to form a base.

The slip needs to be a fairly thin, creamy consistency, and should be sprayed on in several thin layers of between 1 and 3mm (⅟₁₆ and ⅛in) thick, rather than trying to apply it too thickly in fewer coats. Each coating should be allowed to dry considerably before the next one is applied, to avoid sagging, or the risk of the wet coat pulling off the underlying one. Small pieces can be rotated to keep the layers even, and they will be self-supporting after two or three coatings. The number of layers needed and the eventual thickness of the clay obviously depends on the size and shape of the finished piece. It takes

A method for large-scale work devised by Lowell Baker. The form (made from foam) is supported in a frame before the paperclay slip is sprayed on. Photo Jackson A. Baker.

Tip
When spraying a large piece, each successive layer of the paperclay slip could be stained with a different vegetable or food dye. This will burn away with no adverse effects, but will help to show areas that are too thin or have been missed. Coloured dyes are also useful in identifying glazes, many of which look the same when they are in the bucket.

experience to judge just how strong the clay is, but a wall should feel rigid when you press it; if it gives or cracks it requires repairing, either with a patch or the addition of further layers.

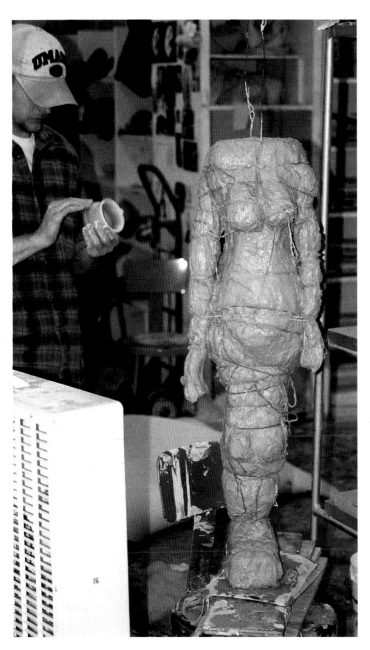

A figurative work by Lowell Baker with string additions for extra strength ready for further spray coating. Photo Jackson A. Baker.

A Metal Framework

The low shrinkage of paperclay (about 2–5 per cent, depending on the recipe) means that even a metal armature need not always be removed before firing if the final temperature is not too high. Over 1000°C shrinkage steadily increases, and at high temperatures (about 1280°C) will be close to that of normal clay.

In California, **LINDA MAU** uses what she describes as 'hardware cloth' – a light steel mesh – to act as the support for her geometric forms. She likes the relationship between art and technology, and her mathematical series uses the shapes of cube, pyramid and rectangle as well as grids. The metal shapes are joined with wire, which also helps to define the form. Paperclay is then either brushed on or poured over, and Linda, too, has found

---

SAFETY

It is essential when doing any spraying that this is done in a controlled environment, away from other people and wearing a mask. Indoors a spray booth or screened off area with extractor fan and good ventilation should be used; outside, care should be taken to avoid any dust blowing towards buildings or damaging plants. A large cardboard carton with one side suitably cut away makes an impromptu spray booth.

When firing foam or polystyrene it must be done in a well-ventilated kiln with adequate ducting to the outside atmosphere as the fumes are potentially hazardous to breathe in; they certainly have an unpleasant smell.

that each layer must be dry before the next one is applied. Once the wire is well covered, the surface is treated with coloured slip or underglaze. There must be sufficient clay in the mix – a ratio of 80 per cent clay to 20 per cent pulp is used – or the work will be too fragile after firing. In the firing, the steel weakens as the clay hardens, adding to the dynamic tension of the work. The firing range of the steel is up to 980°C, and bisqued pieces are smoked with newspaper in an open tub before being waxed and polished. Work that is to be sited outdoors is sealed with a masonry sealer.

Obviously such low-tech methods work best when only one or two similar shapes are wanted; however, they do allow ideas to be tried out quickly and fairly spontaneously, although none of these formers can be thought of as permanent.

Spraying paperclay with an inexpensive sandblaster, Lowell Baker.

Supporting Hollow Forms

Hollow clay forms can be supported with blocks or wedges of foam to keep them upright in the early stages, and large platter-like pieces may be made by rolling out a clay sheet on a cloth and then hanging it up like a hammock from the underside of a bench, shelf, or an upended stool. When using paperclay it is even possible to cast to the required thickness straight on to the cloth (laid on top of a plaster slab or wodge of paper to absorb the surplus water), then when the clay has stiffened sufficiently, to suspend the whole thing without any rolling out at all. This will give a pleasing deckle edge and, depending on the type of cloth used, the weave can also provide an interesting texture; feet or base supports can be added when the clay is hard enough for the whole to be taken down and the cloth peeled away. Clay, even paperclay, shrinks a bit as it dries, and within a hollow mould will pull away from the sides so that the form can be easily released and lifted out. There is no problem with cracking so long as there are no undercuts.

Very Large Scale

A large-scale plaster mould made by Claudi Casanovas during a demonstration at a potters' festival in Wales. This one measured about 1.2m (4ft) in diameter, and was made in less than an hour.

CLAUDI CASANOVAS believes that 'there is an engineering solution to every problem', and the scale of the work he creates certainly poses problems in mould-making. He solves them in an amazing way.

His moulds begin as a double skin of strong polythene sheet firmly attached to the top of a floor-standing wooden frame. The desired shape is marked out, and the two plastic sheets heat-sealed together along the line. All joins are securely sealed, except for a small aperture for an air-hose. The 'mould' is then blown up to the required curve like an enormous balloon – some are 1.5m (5ft) across – and kept at the right pressure with bursts from the air pump if there is any sign of deflating.

A layer of clay is then quickly laid over the plastic surface. Since the finished work will

be heavily textured there is no need for a very smooth surface. The clay is followed by a layer of plaster built up and spread over till thick enough, with scrim soaked in plaster acting as a reinforcement. At this juncture a relay of helpers mixing successive buckets of plaster is a necessity. When dry, the mould is cleverly reversed by turning over onto a board the whole wooden frame to which the plastic is fixed, and the clay can then be pulled away from inside the hollow form. The mould is still huge – this is not a method for the delicate – but it is much thinner and less weighty than might be supposed.

Plaster Moulds

Making a plaster mould implies a certain commitment: a good deal of effort is required to make satisfactory moulds, even simple one-piece ones turned on a lathe, so it does not make sense to go to such trouble unless they are going to be used for repeat works and to last for some time. Complex shapes will require moulds made in several sections that fit accurately together, particularly if the object is to be slipcast. Piece moulds can be used for hand-building if slabs are pressed into each

*R*oy Ashmore packing a mould with straw soaked in coloured slips. The clay may remain in the former for up to four weeks before being removed for firing. A similar method was used for the bust illustrated in Chapter 9, where parts of the surface were broken away after firing.

section, then assembled as each part becomes stiff enough.

To make a plaster mould, the prototype is placed on a board or sheet of glass and surrounded by a wall of clay (if it is a small piece) or a material such as linoleum or flexible plastic sheet (called a cottle) for larger work. This is positioned a few centimetres away from the shape, and high enough to allow the form to be completely covered to the same depth. The cottle should be tied firmly with string, or held with rubber bands cut from inner tubes to prevent it unrolling or being pushed out of shape by the plaster, and all joins must be sealed with clay, particularly around the base to stop the plaster running out. A sufficient amount of plaster is then mixed and poured in gently, making sure that all the clay model is well covered, and that no air pockets are allowed to develop.

The plaster will harden in only a few minutes, creating considerable heat as it

---

Tip

Clay used to make plaster moulds should never be returned to the clay bin for further use: it must always be kept separate, although it can be used again for other work with plaster so long as it is not fired. It will contain minute particles of lime which are hygroscopic – meaning they absorb water, which causes them to swell, even years later in a fired piece. This pushes off the glaze or outer surface and leaves a crater in which the white, chalky granules can easily be seen.

---

does so, and once firm enough the cottle can be pulled away, the whole mould turned over and the original prototype pulled out. At this stage the plaster is still soft and easily damaged, so any small fragments of clay still sticking to it are best left until the plaster stiffens some more, by which time the clay will also have dried and will be easy to brush off without risk of marking the surface.

On an Architectural Scale

The relatively low-tech methods so far described are not possible for the large-scale architectural work that **FELICITY AYLIEFF** creates, and she has developed methods to suit her individual requirements. Every detail needs careful planning – the quantities of materials required, the speed of working, the equipment needed for moving heavy pieces – including measuring the width of doorways and the size of the kiln. However, it is important to her that the objects are not considered merely for their scale, but rather for their sense of volume, fluency and clarity of form. She says: 'I am drawn to forms that are bold, simple and often stark, which may appear quiet and unassuming, but are arresting through their powerful presence.' She describes her references as being to architecture and the natural world – 'the reflection of underlying form through surface articulation and structure' – and the objects themselves as identifying more with their environment, interior or exterior, than relating to past ceramic traditions.

*S*piral by Felicity Aylieff. This complex piece was made from a many-sectioned mould using the methods described in this chapter.

Drawing natural forms of seeds, pods and fruits gave her an understanding of structure which, combined with an interest in early Indian sculpture, motivated an important body of work. These forms were not vehicles for additional surface decoration, and the aim was to achieve an overall simplicity, where the visual texture, though restrained, was an integral part of each piece. Glass and fired chips of coloured porcelain are used as aggregates in the clay matrix, the glass giving areas of transparency and depth to otherwise dense masses of clay. The finished surfaces are designed to be left unglazed, and are ground and polished to a smooth, gleaming refinement, needing no other coating to distract from the random qualities of the aggregates.

Methods and Materials

To start with, making small maquettes helped to define the objects from all angles, and to anticipate possible problems before moving on to the large moulds. Sections were scaled up and cut from styrofoam, then individual pieces cemented together to create the full-sized model. At this stage the foam shape is larger than the finished model will be in order to allow for further refinement. The styrofoam is worked on in detail with hand saw, surforms, files and an electric carving knife to achieve the subtleties of the finished form, and final smoothing is done with sandpaper for a good surface. The whole model is finally covered with two coats of emulsion paint to seal the surface and make it less vulnerable to damage.

In making the mould sections from the model, each one had to be of a size that could be handled, that had no undercuts, and allowed access for joints and seams to be made. In order to keep the weight as light as possible, a splash-moulding technique was used and a thin, shell-like coating of plaster applied first, followed by a layer of a thicker mix incorporating scrim to give extra strength. Each part of the form needed to be moulded separately, with the sections carefully masked off and natches attached at intervals to provide location points, and adjacent sections soft soaped to prevent them sticking together. The mould for one particular form required fourteen separate pieces, and was designed for the sections to release off a spiral and be self-supporting when assembled.

White Vingerling and unrefined brick clays are used, to which pellets of ballontini and borosilicate glass and fragments of fired, brightly coloured porcelain are added.

The outer layer contains a higher proportion of both grog and aggregates, and is slapped into the mould in soft, hand-sized pads with a slight overlay which then need very little further thinning. The backing layer is finer, containing less aggregate, making it easier to apply, and solving the shrinkage differential. To prevent the clay drying out too fast the plaster is saturated with water and sections sprayed from time to time. The clay may remain in the moulds for up to two weeks. The leather-hard form is then supported on a cushion of foam and takes six to eight weeks to dry out thoroughly, at first being wrapped in a jacket of newsprint to even out the drying, and later being moved to a warm room before firing.

In the kiln, objects are placed on a blanket of ceramic fibre. They are once-fired very slowly in an electric kiln, taking about fifty hours to reach a temperature of 1020°C. Final polishing is a major procedure for which a variety of special tools have been adapted: an electric grinder is water-fed to eliminate dust and lubricate the surface, and interchangeable diamond discs are used with it, with pads for the final refinement, giving a smooth and gleaming surface.

Rotation by Felicity Aylieff, details as opposite. This picture clearly shows the combination of aggregates, and their different sizes, used in the body.

14 Print and Paint

From the beginning, decoration should be thought of as an integral part of any piece, and never just as something applied to the surface as an afterthought, whether it be a coloured glaze or a more elaborate printed or painted pattern. Traditionally, printed decoration on objects made from clay has had rather a cheap, mass-produced image probably deriving from the on-glaze transfers used in great numbers on factory-made ware. The making of these transfer decals, and particularly the engraved metal plates they are printed from, is a highly skilled job, but the implied link with a repetitive industrial process has not been one that studio potters have wanted to be associated with until recently, when improved printing and photographic techniques have enabled them to create their own.

'In Memory of...' by Claire Redwood. Lino-cut and silk-screen prints on porcelain paperclay. Many images collaged and assembled in mould. Fired to 1260°C.

Printing is normally done onto a flat surface, and ceramics are usually in the round, so linking the two- and three-dimensional aspect is the first technical problem to be solved by anyone wanting to decorate in this way. An image on a non-flat surface appears differently to one seen straight on, and sometimes several images will be viewed simultaneously, meeting up as they surround a form.

The methods described here are for printing on a flat surface, but the capacity of paperclay to alter from wet to dry and back again means that the printing can be done on a dry flat sheet that is later – months later if need be – damped and softened before being cut to shape to make a three-dimensional piece, or formed using a mould.

Unfired paperclay can be rolled so thin and is so strong that it lends itself easily to most normal methods of printing. When allowed to dry out it is more like a thick, handmade paper than clay, and at that stage can virtually be used as a paper. It should still retain a hint of inner moisture however, so that the sheet can be handled safely and does not crumble under pressure if put through in a press. The exact state of dryness/dampness must be learned from experience, added to knowledge of the particular materials being use and the techniques employed.

Preparing the Surface

Paperclay tends to have a slightly lumpy surface, so if it is to be printed with images requiring fine detail it will have either to be rolled more smoothly, or to have the surface coated with a finer slip.

Rolling is a good way to thin a sheet which is too thick, compressing the body and strengthening it at the same time, and possibly also making it more flexible in the process. It will also smooth the top surface and texture the lower one with whatever the clay sheet is lying on. Paperclay slip which is intended to be made into sheets for printing can be mixed and spread more thinly than usual, but it is my belief that making the original slab slightly too thick and then rolling it makes a stronger sheet than casting thin, because the compression helps to align and bond the clay particles together.

Covering with a layer of slip can also even out irregularities, though it depends how this is done. Several thin coats sprayed on will give a fine surface for printing, and the addition of coloured stain will add another dimension if different colours are used for each layer and certain areas masked off to complement the eventual printing. Both sides of a clay sheet can be treated at once if a plaster slab first has a slip coating brushed or sprayed on, or a design applied with a slip trailer before the paperclay is laid over the top and the upper surface rolled and coloured. This can be useful when both sides of a sheet will be visible, as in a vase or dish for example, although care will need to be taken to avoid smudging the surfaces when joining sections together.

Monoprinting

It is possible to elaborate on the process described above, in a version of monoprinting where a whole design can be built up on a smooth board or slightly damp plaster slab. Layers of colour from slips or stains may be brushed or sprayed on, with finer detail made by brush strokes, slip trailing, or even by cutting away using a sgraffito technique if the layers are thick enough. It must be remembered, however, that the top layer seen on the plaster slab will become the one attached to the paperclay when the clay sheet is laid on top, and will therefore become the background of the design, i.e. the design must be applied in reverse. When the design is complete, a sheet of clay is carefully laid over it and firmly and evenly rolled all over the back to pick up the image. The paperclay slab is then carefully pulled away from the plaster. Enough of the underlying design may remain to take further 'prints', or more details can be added to change each image slightly, making subtle differences as a series is developed.

Images can be stretched and distorted by picking the clay sheet up and slapping the whole thing down onto the work surface several times. This can give an interesting effect, though it takes some practice to achieve just the right degree of alteration without the sheet tearing apart or sticking in a wrinkled mass to the bench: it is all to easy to be left holding only two small corners. Having the paperclay damp enough to be flexible but not too soggy helps, and the sheet must be thicker than normal so that the stretching does not thin it too drastically. The effect is more pleasing than simply rolling the clay, which tends to make the surface flat and the image look a bit squashed.

Photocopying

In his book *Ceramics and Print* Paul Scott describes in detail many of the printing techniques that he and others have developed successfully; one in particular of these is now in very common usage. It requires a photocopier which can be stopped and opened before the print has gone through the heat-sealing process: at this stage the image is

'Last Thoughts' by Helen Smith. Porcelain paperclay with photocopy print and smoked lettering; one piece from an installation exhibited in 1998. The skulls were made from porcelain paperclay, and each was printed with a sepia portrait, inspired by graveyard photographs seen on tombs in France. Inside each are the hypothetical last words of the person written in smoke. Finally each skull bowl is encrusted with salt, giving a crystalline surface, and having overtones of salt glazing, preservation, and the sea.

made from a fine coating of toner powder which has been electrically charged so that it sticks to the surface of the paper. The image can be carefully transferred by laying the paper face down on the surface of the clay, and gently but firmly rolling the back of the paper to press the toner onto the clay. At this stage it is also possible to alter the photocopied image by blurring or rubbing off parts of the dusty surface before pressing it onto the clay.

Toners contain oxides, mainly iron, so the image may then fire successfully onto the clay surface, giving a sepia-toned effect, though this depends on the type being used. Sometimes the image may apparently disappear during the bisque firing; however, it will magically reappear if the clay is brushed over with underglaze stain and then wiped clean with a sponge. The colour will remain in the photocopied lines if the initial pressing has been clear enough, and the image can then be further developed, and enhanced with extra colours, before being glazed and fired again. Several photocopies can also be laid one overlapping the other to give very complex layers of imagery.

Stamps and Sponges

The idea behind these is simple, though they may be built up into intricate designs, with one pattern or colour layered upon another.

Sponges

These decorate the clay surface by adding a layer of colour from slip, stain or glaze. The texture of a particular piece of natural sponge may give enough background pattern if dipped in stain and dabbed over the surface; or manufactured foam, which has a denser, more even texture, can easily be cut into a variety of shapes. One colour can be laid over another, and one pattern be superimposed on another; however, they do not basically alter the underlying clay surface. Because they are simple they are often associated with peasant pottery, particularly Scottish, where copper green,

'Crossed Lines' by Anne Lightwood. Porcelain paperclay with slips; nine panels laid flat for painting using coloured sprays, stencils, sponges and brushwork. Unfired.

iron browns and a range of purples from manganese were often used. In early work it was the root of the sponge (which has a denser texture) that was mostly used, and pieces of it were tied with thread and bound into the shapes required. The oxide tended to run and blur in the firing, so of necessity the image was stylized. Today, many potters use upholstery foam which has a close texture and can be cut with a sharp blade, an electric carving knife or a heated wire. If the latter method is used a mask should be worn because the burning foam gives off fumes as it melts.

Stamps

These are made from more durable material than sponges and, being harder, usually leave an indentation in the surface of the clay. Colour can be transferred by rolling slip or stain over the surface of the stamps before pressing them down on the clay, though sometimes no further decoration is needed since the pooling of glaze in the hollows gives sufficient variation.

Alternatively, stain or oxide can be brushed on to different areas of the impressed clay once it has been bisqued, and the surplus wiped away so that the colour remains only in the hollows that have been stamped. This method can also be used over quite large areas if they have been textured by rolling out on a coarse cloth, for instance. Pressing a sheet of softish clay all over with a crumpled pad of newspaper is also surprisingly effective if the creases are later emphasized with colour. The carved wooden blocks used for Indian textile printing are now widely available and found in many potters' toolboxes.

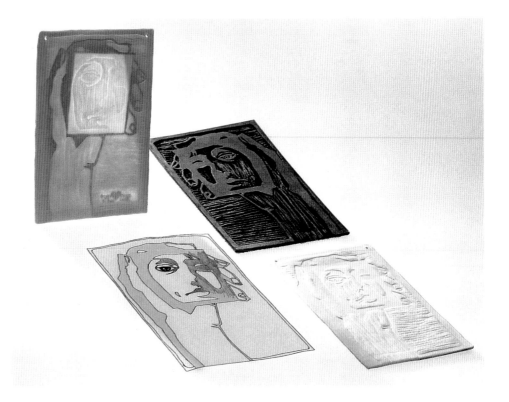

*L*ino blocks and prints by Frederick Payne. The picture shows the original cut lino block with the images made by it; within fired, coloured clay sheet; printed on paper, and embossed on to soft clay.

Lino blocks are also used by several artists, either to print with directly in the conventional way, when the surface may be coloured but only slightly embossed; or by pressing a thin piece of clay onto the lino – without any ink – to create different thicknesses in the clay; this gives a shadowed effect if the clay is thin enough to be translucent.

Family Album

CLAIRE REDWOOD has used lino cuts in combination with other techniques to create a unique memorial to a family she has known only from reminiscence and various inherited fragments. Coming from a German-Jewish background, and scattered as refugees by the Holocaust, many relatives were imprisoned and died in camps; but neither Nazism or Judaism was ever mentioned during her childhood. In her current work she is trying to express the hidden layers of what was left unsaid. She says:

All the work could not have been made without paperclay. The ripped edge unique to paperclay and the collaging of printed images would have been fraught with difficulties if made with clay alone. For some work the paperclay was first completely dry for silk-screening, then damp for etching and lino cut. The ability to join wet to dry was vital when a large number of prints had first to be amassed to compile a work. Some, the lino cuts, were wet, and others dry – the silk screened images. The ragged edges, the peeled look of paperclay that lends itself to collaging and the layering of images are areas I intend to develop and explore.

'*Fragment 1*' by *Claire Redwood. Silk screen print on stoneware paperclay fired to 1200°C. 18 × 21 × 5cm (7 × 8 × 2in).*

Claire also finds paperclay excellent for printing as it absorbs the ink so well and when dry does not seem to stick to the screens: when re-wetted the ink does not seem to run. The paperclay sheet peels easily from a lino block or etching plate, and its inherent strength means that any tears can be repaired easily. The lino cuts are printed directly onto paperclay using stains or oxides mixed with fat oil or copper plate oil, and the prints are then pressed into moulds to form wall-hung tablets. Silk-screened text and images and embossed textures are also torn up and collaged together within the moulds, the crowding of images reflecting the herding together of refugees and massed camp inmates, while the lettering refers to the scant lists and records left behind.

Intaglio

The word 'intaglio' has come to mean a 'surface which has been cut into or engraved'. It describes the conventional copperplate printing technique where ink is rolled onto an engraved metal plate, and the surface is wiped clean, with the ink remaining only in the parts which have been cut away (unlike the previous methods where the colour is printed from the raised areas). Damp paper is then placed over the plate and the whole is put through a press, forcing the paper into the grooves where it picks up the ink. After pressing, the paper is carefully peeled back and lifted off. Obviously this technique cannot be used with normal clay, so previously the metal plate had to be used to print onto an intermediate flexible surface such as a gelatine pad which was then used to transfer the image to the clay surface. But with paperclay this is not a problem, and the sheet of paperclay can be used exactly like printing paper, passing it through the press so that the print is impressed directly onto it.

This is the method used by **LOTTE GLOB** for printing the copper plate etchings for the pages in her series of ceramic 'books', although she makes two alterations: first, she passes the paperclay sheet through the press before putting in the inked plate; this is to smooth the surface of the clay, and the dryness/dampness of the sheet is a critical factor at this stage. She also substitutes newspaper padding for the usual blanket above and below the plate: this is to absorb any extra moisture and to avoid any crumbles of clay inadvertently being left in the press.

ROBERT TASKER is another who favours this method, although he is unusual in that he uses his clay very soft, like dough, when he makes an intaglio print, so the clay is still sufficiently pliable for the shape to be bent or curved after printing.

PAUL SCOTT has devised an even simpler method which does not need a press. A design is drawn onto a plaster slab and carved out while the plaster has still not quite hardened off. At this stage it is easy to obtain a range of thicknesses of line and different textures with simple carving tools. The plaster must then dry out thoroughly, after which it can be used to print from, either used as a plate with ink in the incised lines, or as a raised relief where the clay has been firmly pressed into the carved surfaces without using stain. A hard type of plaster should be used to make the block last longer, and to show up finer detail in the carving; but even so, a plaster slab will still crack if put through a press.

WILLIAM HALL uses a version of this technique, with a low-relief image carved on a plaster slab in place of the metal plate, and coloured slip as ink. The slip is poured or brushed onto the slab, then carefully cleaned back to reveal the image. (A slightly damp plaster slab will accept the slip more easily.) A cottle is then put around the image, and thin casting slip containing 200 mesh molochite is poured over it. A second backing layer of thicker slip including a coarser grade of molochite follows, and when stiff enough the

Copper etching by Lotte Glob. Printed on paperclay sheet.

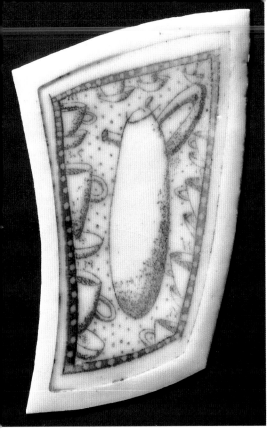

'Tea Time' by Paul Scott, 1994. Etching on HF porcelain paperclay fired to 1200°C. Printed with cobalt and copper ink and covered with transparent glaze. 10 × 15cm (4 × 6in). Photo Andrew Morris (left).

Detail from 'In Memory of...' by Claire Redwood. This shows clearly the variety of techniques used for a complex image, and the number of pieces included (below).

cottle is removed and the print carefully eased from the plaster.

Silk Screening

This is another technique where the concept is simple but the results achieved can be sophisticated and satisfying. A frame of wood or metal has a screen of fine mesh stretched tightly over it so that the material is taut, and printing ink is pushed through the mesh with a rubber-edged tool called a squeegee. Originally the material used was silk, hence the name, but now man-made fibres such as nylon or polyester are used. The size of the mesh – the number of threads per inch or cm – is a crucial factor: with a coarse weave, too much ink is likely to get through, causing bleeding or blotches, but if it is too fine the particles in the ink will not be able to pass through and the screen will become blocked so that some areas will not print. The size of the mesh should be a little larger than the granule size (about 110/120 threads per inch as a guide), so matching the screen mesh size to the size of the granules in the ink is important.

Areas of the screen will have to be blanked off to make the design, and this can be done very simply with paper stencils or masking tape. It is a little more complicated to paint the screen using a suitable blocking medium – this means choosing oil for water or vice versa, so that the ink will not cause the masking medium to dissolve. Fine or detailed images can be drawn first with pencil or pen and ink, then photocopied onto acetate film, from which the images can be transferred photographically onto a screen for printing.

Using photographic techniques will give the best results for fine line and complex designs, but they require specialized equipment and materials usually found in colleges or printshops, but not in most ceramic workshops. The process involves the screen being treated to render it photosensitive, then being exposed to ultraviolet light, the image developed from an opaque 'positive', and the unexposed areas washed away with lukewarm water. The positive may be a photocopy or drawing on acetate, a high-contrast film positive, or any flat object such as a leaf or a feather which has different densities and opaque areas. This is also the method used for printing decal transfers where the images are printed onto special paper and covered with a film known as a covercoat. Transfers are made in huge numbers industrially and can be bought off the shelf, but individual potters also make their own. The images are floated off the covercoat onto the fired, glazed surface of the piece and are then fired at a lower temperature to fix them. They can be applied to a curved or an upright surface.

Another alternative technique suggested by Robert Tasker is to screenprint onto a smooth plaster slab, then cast paperclay slip over it. The slip will pick up the screen print and the resulting sheet will be pliable enough to be used almost as a textile, the image stretched or distorted if it is further rolled or bent.

'Children of Kosovo' by Shirley Eccles, 1999. Porcelain paperclay panels printed using decals made by the artist from photographic images.

Making a Statement

SHIRLEY ECCLES is a South African now living in England, and she has chosen on-glaze printing using her own decals as her method for a piece of work called 'Children of Kosovo'. This is a contemporary issue, but is not meant primarily as a political statement, rather as an exploration of the trauma any such children face on being torn from the security of home and country. Her own country has a very high crime rate, and the violence, death and fear that such young people have experienced has robbed them of their youth. Such images appear so often in the press that we are in danger of becoming inured to them, but still they plead to be recognized.

Method and Materials

Porcelain has been chosen for its colour and translucency, and the delicate nature of the thin tiles relates to the fragility of the children. The tiles were made by compressing paper porcelain between two porous bats; each one is about 12 by 16cm (5 × 6in). The bisque firing was to 1000°C, and the second, with a transparent glaze, to 1280°C. The decals were screened onto Unical paper sealed with covercoat; these were then transferred to a glazed tile and refired to 800°C.

Preparing screens photographically along with various different printing methods is well described in specialized books, and there is not space here to go into great detail; but the possibilities for using paperclay with printing techniques are exciting, and only just beginning to be explored fully.

Ceramic Inks

The ingredients used to make a ceramic printing ink are metallic oxides and commercially made stains that are generally coarser than those used for normal printing inks; first of all, therefore, it is necessary to grind materials as fine as possible with a muller or palette knife on a glass slab before combining them with whatever binding medium is to be used.

Detail from Kosovo panel by Shirley Eccles. Printed from transfer decal.

Stains are often manufactured to a finer grade than oxides, and catalogues will give a mesh size (this is the size of sieve that they will pass through). Oxides are coarser, but a carbonate may have a smaller grain size and be more easily dispersed in a slip or printing ink while giving the same colour effect. The colour must be blended with a medium which may be either oil- or water-based.

The ink used by Lotte Glob is either cobalt or manganese, or a combination of both, ground on a glass slab and mixed with fat oil or printer's ink oil. Claire Redwood uses two parts of black stain to one part of fat oil for lino printing, and two parts black body stain to one part silk screen medium for screening. Paul Scott's ink is made from ten parts underglaze colour, five parts sieved clay and ten parts textile printing medium, ground on a glass slab to the right consistency. Further medium can be used to extend the ink. Transfers are made in the same way, but using powdered glaze instead of clay, and printing onto decal paper with oil-based medium, then covering with covercoat.

Oil-based systems have been proved to be extremely reliable, but the solvents needed both for printing and to clean the screens cause problems, and water-based methods are now becoming more commonly used. Printers, like those working in other media, are increasingly aware of the hazards of many chemicals frequently in use, and new water-based systems provide a safer solution. Manufacturers are continually working to produce improved ingredients, and their catalogues are regularly updated with details of new developments.

Painting

In my own work, paperclay is frequently used like a canvas or cartridge paper, as a base for spraying or brushwork, and the images are almost always abstract, often derived from signs and symbols, and using strong colours. The slip is porcelain, the same as that used to make the paperclay but sieved through a much finer mesh to prevent the spraygun becoming blocked. Usually there are many layers of colour, with areas masked out using torn paper or a selection of stencils cut from card which can be overlaid and resprayed in dozens of different ways. Smaller sponges and stamps are worked in, and further detail added by slip trailing or brushwork. This is all done while the pieces are flat, and usually a series is painted together, allowing time for layers to dry sufficiently before placing stencils on top, to avoid smudging and spoiling the surface. There is no problem with the work drying out, even if the painting is spread over several days: just laying the paperclay on a damp cloth seems to allow it to absorb sufficient moisture to remain pliable enough to press over a hump mould when the painting is complete. However, at this stage care must be taken to ensure that the top has dried enough to be pressed onto the mould without sticking, and thereby damaging the painted surface. The work is unglazed, and once-fired to 1260°C; it is finished by polishing with beeswax to seal the surface.

'Crossed Lines' by Anne Lightwood, 1997: the nine-piece panel after being once-fired to 1260°C; from a series called 'Put Out More Flags'. The work refers to flags and emblems and the ways in which the meaning of 'the colours' can be used to rouse loyalty, or to conceal the mayhem of battle. 1 × 1m (3.3 × 3.3ft).

15 Playing with Fire

There has always been a mystique about kilns and firing, one that has no doubt grown from the universal fascination most people feel for the dangers and attractions of fire, whether it be a roaring garden bonfire or logs smouldering comfortingly in the grate. This excitement and unpredictability has been rather damped for many potters in recent years by the bland efficiency of electric kilns and computerized controllers. However much of a relief it is to pack a kiln, set the controls and go home for the night leaving technology to get on with it, for many it cannot compete with the life and death struggle of stoking a kiln for hours (or days) on end until the desired temperature is achieved. It doesn't seem quite real, somehow, just to press a switch.

Having said that, modern materials allow today's potter to think laterally and have the best of both worlds, linking high- and low-tech by using fire in different ways. Many now use an electric or gas kiln for initial firings, then turn to raku techniques or a low temperature smoke firing to achieve their final effects. These methods are particularly suitable for

Detail of raku-fired Armour piece by Sara Challinor. The work is fired to 800°C and very quickly transferred to a smoking bin and covered with sawdust in order to achieve a highly reduced surface.

paperclay, since even after firing to a stoneware temperature it will retain a certain degree of porosity, allowing the smoke to penetrate the pores. Moreover, much (most?) of the work being made in paperclay is not functional in the sense of having to stand up to dishwashers or hot domestic ovens, so firing to a lower temperature poses no problem – unless the work is to be sited out of doors, when it must be sealed with a waterproof coating. Also, many makers no longer use glaze, preferring to stain or texture the surface of the clay, enhancing the surface by waxing and polishing after treating with wet and dry carborundum papers; therefore reaching a specific temperature to mature a glaze is no longer an essential, either.

Firing

Nevertheless, certain strictures still need to be applied, however forgiving the material. The temperature rise must be slow enough to allow evaporation to take place gradually, and it also helps to warm the piece through gently before the real firing begins. Placing work close to, or on top of, the kiln during the previous firing is one easy way to do this, as long as it can be done safely – obviously work should not be positioned where it will be knocked, or left in a hot spot near a bung or spy hole where there is a risk of any one part being exposed to sudden bursts of heat. Packing the next firing straight into a warm kiln as soon as it has been emptied is another safety idea, even when the firing proper will not start for some hours or even days: the heat is there and it has already been paid for, so it makes sense to make as much use of it as possible.

However, because of the large amounts of combustible materials included in paper-clay and other fibre-type mixes, these give off very large amounts of smoke and fumes at an early part of the firing – around 260°C. This means that adequate ventilation both of the kiln and of the room in which it is housed is essential. With an electric kiln and modern controllers it may be possible to set these so that firing begins at night when it is less likely to cause problems within the workshop or with neighbours, but bungs which have been left open to vent the fumes must then be closed to allow the firing to continue efficiently. Timing is therefore important. A gas-, oil-, or wood-fired kiln will already have a flue or chimney so the products of combustion can more easily be vented safely outside, but the atmosphere within the workshop must still be considered. Once the paper or other material has burned out, the firing schedule can be continued as normal for the type of clay being used and the final effect desired.

For some potters, sculptors, or 'artists in fire' as they might be described, the kiln has actually become the sculpture. That is, it is no longer made as a box to contain heat in order to raise the temperature sufficiently to fire pots contained within it, but it is seen as a work of creation in its own right. The piece is fired from within by a fire set inside it, rather than being enveloped in flame from the outside. The kiln is no longer a means to an end, but an end in itself, and the action of the flames is necessary for the piece to come alive. Work created in this way may be strong enough to survive afterwards if a high enough temperature has been reached, or it may be allowed to decay gradually as a further part of the process, the outer, less-fired areas dissolving first.

Dragons and Fire Trees

WALI HAWES describes these as 'Fired Earth Constructions' (one is illustrated in Chapter 2), and he has been experimenting in this way for years with increasing degrees of success, the constructions becoming more sophisticated with experience. Beginning with a group of decorated bottle kilns built from adobe bricks, the work developed into

'The Legendary Tower of Babel', 1999; a sculpture built as a kiln by Malgorzata Dyrda-Kujawska of Poland at a potters' festival in Wales. The work warming through with a small fire (right) *and with the fibre blanket in place before firing proper begins* (far right).

'Fire Trees' and 'Fire Flowers' – these were a series of structures, basically chimneys, with the firebox set in the base and the whole acting as an updraught kiln. The flame pouring from the top and from smaller flues built out from the sides became the 'branches'. A technically incorrect ratio between wide firebox and narrow flue meant that a reducing atmosphere was created within the structure, producing long tongues of flame when the damper was opened or adjusted. The fire trees were dramatic and fun, built in a spirit of fiesta in a day or two from adobe clay and decorated on the outside with coloured slips and oxides. Open-bodied clay containing chopped straw, sometimes with a clay content as little as 40 per cent, was made into blocks like unfired bricks and used to build with. The raw fire-pieces may weigh two or three tons, so finding the right balance is a consideration, as is judging the correct degree of dampness. The drying process is usually quick, but there are problems with the structure cracking if the firing is too rapid.

A 'Dragon Kiln' made for a festival in Ono, Japan was successful, but was not allowed to remain *in situ* very long because a year later the authorities wanted to put a car park on the site, even though it was still in perfect condition. This echoes the problems other potters find with their work, particularly when it is on a large scale. If it does not fit into an easily understood convention, it is simpler to ignore it or to get rid of it.

A Fire-Breathing Dragon

The dragon was called Yoko – as the obvious complement to Ono – and it was built from a local mountain clay normally used for roof tiles; the paper came in compressed recycled sheets from a factory, and first had to be roughly pulped down. The pulp was added to the moistened clay at the clay works, blended by hand, and then plugged until one ton of paperclay was prepared.

The making was mainly coiling, with the initial tail stages being supported on a bamboo framework. This was not found to be strong enough for the body, which was entirely coiled in a conventional way. Working to a deadline meant continuing through a typhoon and rainstorm, but lighting a small fire inside the body helped the drying-out process, and the whole dragon was completed in three days. Paperclay was found to be excellent for the job and additions easy to make, though a longer drying period of up to two weeks would have made firing easier, as this had to begin when the clay was still very damp.

Firing was begun at 6am, and twelve hours later flame was spouting dramatically from the mouth, bellowing smoke and sparks. Waste wood containing a high proportion of resin was used, to give flame rather than heat, since the structure was to be fired on the inside only, and was not intended to be permanent.

*'B*uilding Yoko': Wali Hawes built this dragon kiln for a festival in Japan. The firebox is in the tail, which has been partially dried by lighting a small fire in it. The clay used was local tile clay mixed with paper waste. Photo Hirani Teremi.

The paperclay was pushed to the limits, and stood up well to the task. It had been chosen because of the difficulty of obtaining the right materials for adobe in Japan, and also because Wali had heard the claims made for paperclay and wanted to test them for himself. He found it better than adobe for large-scale pieces, and though the fired ceramic material is slightly weaker physically, there was no problem with sections spalling off, as had been found with previous clays. Wali describes himself as an anarchic potter who enjoys being controversial if it makes the onlooker question assumptions and think in a different way. He describes Japan as being a supportive environment for potters, where their skills are given serious appreciation – so long as their work can be considered within existing conventions. Building Yoko was really to prove that unlikely materials can meet the challenge, and to unite the spectators in the excitement and drama of fire.

A Forest Refuge

HANNAH AYRE is also addicted to fire, seeing her firings as a performance that draws the onlookers in and links them in an almost hypnotic experience. But the structures she creates are intended ultimately to be quiet and meditative, rich in visual textures and associations, made literally from the surrounding earth and trees. Her latest work is a series of shelters

The dragon alight. The clay has changed colour as the structure dries out (above). *Photo Hirani Teremi.*

The final stage at night. Wood containing a high proportion of resin was used to give flame and sparks rather than great heat. Photo Hirani Teremi.

Garden kiln by Hannah Ayre, 1997. This was built over a structure of fallen branches using local clays mixed with elements from the surrounding area such as pine needles.

along a forest trail in which walkers can rest and sit, each a tranquil place to think and to be alone. She feels that art can have a huge impression on people when they are physically involved with it: 'If they are inside a sculpture they become part of it.'

The work is built and fired *in situ*, with the materials coming from the site as much as is possible, and specific to it. During construction the clay is supported by a structure of branches which dictates where and how the clay should lie. The clay is often scrap brick clay, with materials such as pine needles mixed in, the local clays being used as outer glazes or coatings. The fuel is wind-blown wood which would otherwise rot away and be wasted, and the firing lasts for about twenty-four hours; in this time the support branches burn away, leaving the imprint of every stick, with traces in the clay like fossils so that the texture is richly patterned and the method of construction clearly seen.

Hannah calls herself an environmental sculptor, and is careful to explain that when wood is burned, it gives off exactly the same amount of carbon dioxide as would be emitted during the much longer process of decomposition. Since only a small amount of ash is left, she does not feel she is adding to the pollution problem. She is interested in natural cycles – seasons, time, tides or drought and the changes they bring – and in recognizing and using the properties of different materials. Clay shrinks and dries, becoming ceramic when it is fired, an irreversible process; wood also shrinks and cracks, burns and decomposes, and the two materials work both with and against each other. Once fired, the pieces are left to the elements to be gradually reclaimed as they decay.

The same kiln during firing.

SculpturKilns

NINA HOLE is a Danish ceramist: she lives in a small village and is influenced by her surroundings, particularly architecture. She is known internationally for her SculpturKilns which she has built in many countries, and from many different clays and materials, but for some time she has also been exploring the possibilities of the house as a form through which to express thoughts or tell stories. She is inspired by the architectural aspect, but says: 'I am also using the house to represent the human being – a human container – the human cover.' Last year as an ironic comment on the difficulties people have with non-functional form she started turning the houses upside down to use as vases or receptacles, and now finds herself making teapots in the form of upside-down houses!

The SculpturKilns are built on the spot as large-scale installations. The idea for them was born when she was invited to develop something new for 'North' – a workshop for graduate students throughout Scandinavia. In appalling weather a group of about thirty students built three towers, each using a different technique and modular construction. The towers were built over a firebox, wrapped in fibre blanket, dried and fired in five days.

Each of her works now is meticulously planned, since each kiln is for a different environment and poses a different set of problems. Many can be solved by thinking ahead, and drawings are the first stage in capturing ideas. Models and templates are made before building begins, to identify possible construction problems and to map out the flow of fire. Nina is adamant that using cheap or scrap clay is a false economy, and says:

> There are certain things you can't compromise on. The clay material is an essential. Even though the amount needed is huge – between two and three tons – the clay must be of a type and quality requested. There is a tendency to use discarded clay or seconds, but that must be discouraged. The failure of a project because of inferior clay is disheartening, and the energy, expectations and effort of everyone involved must be remembered.

'S*culpturKiln' by Nina Hole. Setting up the template for one of Nina's kilns at Charlottenborg, Copenhagen in 1998. She makes very detailed plans before starting to build, aiming to eliminate structural problems later on.*

A*lmost at the top: building the Charlottenborg kiln. The sculpture had a straight tower 4m (13ft) high with a serrated tail-form to add lightness and fantasy. The picture shows very clearly the U-shaped configuration of the blocks made for the construction. Their interlocking shape makes the wall very strong.*

She is not fond of local brick clay, preferring a strong, well grogged body (from 30–40 per cent grog) to which sawdust or paper is added.

A SculpturKiln is by no means a perfect kiln, though it is designed to function both as kiln and chimney, and must also be visually pleasing; thus each one will include something new and unique to that event. Nina tries to be versatile, adapting to the differing time scale, organization and aspirations of each situation. Some pieces may be dismantled to be reassembled in a new location, but kilns are not made in great numbers so each one is given thought and careful consideration. Even good ideas may be changed in the building, and the possibility of failure accepted philosophically.

The building method is frequently a module system using U-shaped slabs, about the size of a small firebrick with one leg longer than the other. These are stacked one on top of the other, with the open ends alternating, and when stacked on edge are very strong. Structures up to 4m (13ft) high have been built in this way, the open weave wall allowing fast drying and quick firing.

Once the structure is ready for firing, fibre blanket is wrapped around the outside and held in place with wires: this helps to even up the temperature, ensuring that the outer surface is also fired. Firing begins gently to allow drying and warming of such a weight of clay before the real intensity builds up. At the final stage once temperature has been reached and maintained for long enough for the whole piece to even out, the wires are cut and the blanket pulled away to reveal the whole glowing sculpture amid a shower of sparks like fireworks. Reduction with wood or sawdust *outside* the kiln can also take place at this stage, adding to the excitement. As it cools, flashing from the flame and subtle markings from smoke will be revealed, enriching the natural colour of the clay.

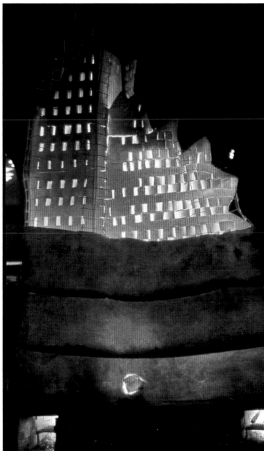

Nina believes that the process is as important as the final product, and that the involvement of a group of people in learning and working together gives each sculpture a unique spirit drawn from each one. Her work has been described as having a contemplative character akin to a Mayan or Hindu temple, and being imbued with a mystical, magic feeling. Nina herself says simply: 'It always amazes me that so many people want to join, work hard and bond with me.'

The day after: flashing from the flame can be seen, and the whole edifice is strong and intact.

*'H*ound Dog' by Ian Gregory; here it is in position in his 'Instant Kiln' made from fibre blanket fixed to metal mesh with ceramic buttons. The dog is built on a kiln shelf, standing on a layer of fibre blanket covered with sand to allow for movement during the firing. The firebox is below, and pieces of shelf act to deflect the direct flame from the dog.

(Almost) Instant Kilns

Making large pieces from paperclay poses special problems when it comes to firing them, but paperclay is so much lighter and stronger than normal that some potters are able to transport their work to large kilns that they can borrow. Others fire their work in sections, cementing it together afterwards; but the really inventive make a kiln to suit the particular needs of the work in hand. **IAN GREGORY'S** sculpted pieces are often built *in situ* and are just too difficult to transport, so he has devised an instant kiln that can be easily adapted to a variety of sizes. The work is built on to a kiln shelf covered with a sheet of fibre blanket with a layer of sand on top. This is to allow the piece to move easily as it shrinks and alters in the firing.

The kiln consists of four separate panels of metal mesh, to which fibre blanket is fixed on the inside. These form the sides of the kiln, and are held together at the corners with jump-lead clips; a top made in the same way is laid over like a lid. A fire port will have been cut in one wall, and a bag wall of suitable height inside protects the work from the direct flame from the burner. The top has an aperture for a flue or a short length of pipe to act as a chimney. The whole thing can be assembled in a few minutes, and by making panels of different sizes, a whole range of kilns to suit particular requirements can easily be put together.

Ian also makes quick raku kilns from Durox insulating building blocks: these are cheap to buy and are laid dry to fit whatever size is needed. They can go up to temperatures of 1100°C and are fired with a single gas burner, being up- or downdraught as desired. A kiln shelf makes a suitable top.

Kiln by Ian Gregory. All four sides are in position. Jump-lead clips hold the sections together, and a further piece acts as a roof.

Bonfire Firings

Pit kilns and bush firings of pots have been used all over the world with greater or lesser success for hundreds of years. The problem is always to raise the temperature sufficiently to fire the clay before the combustible material burns completely away, and to ensure as even a firing as possible without too much sudden flaring, and without any sudden increase of heat that would damage the pots.

Usually a slight hollow or depression is made in the ground, and sometimes a pit is dug. This is covered with a layer of sticks or rice straw or whatever material is being used for fuel, and the pots are carefully stacked on their sides or rims on top of this. Loose fuel is pushed between pieces, and a stack built up in layers with larger pieces at the bottom, and smaller in between and on top. Sometimes large shards and pieces of broken pot are placed on top as an outer layer. The whole mound is then covered over with more fuel, and lit. Care is taken to cover over parts that burn too fiercely with earth or more fuel, and the pots will have been laid to allow air spaces so that combustion can be as even as possible. Some firings may last only a few minutes, others last much longer, and after the main firing is complete the clamp is covered with earth to allow it to cool slowly.

Paper Kilns

Many years ago as a part of a college course at Farnham some students set fire to a structure they had built from rolled up newspaper. The experiment was not to do with kilns, but the structure generated so much heat that it set **SEBASTIAN BLACKIE** thinking about the possibilities, remembering other fast firings that he had seen. He was curious to know whether paper could act both as insulation and as fuel in the same way that other natural materials have been found to do.

His method was to roll up two or three thicknesses of newspaper together into long tubes, slightly wider at one end than the other, and fix them with sticky tape. Then by pushing the thin end of one into the wider end of another, lengths up to ten or twelve feet (3 or 4m) could be made. These were plaited and twisted into rings about 36cm (14in) in diameter, and stacked to form a tapering cylinder roughly 50cm (20in) high. Extra coils were wound around the walls, making them about 5cm (2in) thick. A thick mat of similarly coiled paper formed a floor, and pinch pots were placed inside on their rims before it was sealed at the top with another smaller mat. The kiln burned slowly at first, but the whole thing was soon engulfed in flame, burning from the outside inwards. In an article published in *Ceramic Review* in 1991 (from which much of this information is taken) Sebastian wrote: 'We began to see through the charred and tangled lattice of paper rolls red hot pots, like rosy eggs surrounded by writhing fiery snakes.' The kiln was still burning strongly with a shorter, hotter flame twenty minutes after lighting, and the whole firing lasted about forty minutes in all. The rings of paper kept their shape almost to the end, although incredibly fragile, and gave soft grey flashmarks to the pots where they had been in contact.

This has since become such a well-known and popular way in schools and colleges of experiencing the excitement of firing that it is hard now to remember what a revolutionary concept it seemed then. No equipment is needed, it is quick and understandable, and even with such a low-tech method as this, temperatures of around 750°C are easily reached. In an urban environment it demonstrates some of the primaeval power of fire.

Another quick kiln devised by Ian Gregory for Raku firing. This one is constructed from Duroc insulating blocks, and can be built to suit the size of the work to be fired.

Tip
The sort of shiny-coated papers used in magazines make even better coils than newspaper as a material for a kiln like this. This may be due to the greater quantity of china clay used in manufacture, making the paper burn more slowly and retain the heat for longer.

Conclusion

It is said that in certain Chinese exams the candidates were not presented with a list of questions to answer, but were given the simple instruction: 'Write what you know'.

The first question this poses is where to start. What does one really *know*, as opposed to just making the assumption that something is so? Does *knowing* mean learning facts that can be proved and verified in the same way as a theorem from geometry? And does knowing even very many facts of that sort mean that *understanding* is correspondingly greater?

Such questions seem almost unanswerable, but they have frequently been posed while writing this book. Like anything else it would seem that a balance is needed, in this case between the necessary factual information in what is hoped will become a useful source book, and, equally, with understanding the thinking that motivates artists to work in a particular way. It is not enough just to list materials and recipes in a purely practical manner. With the variety of work currently being produced in ceramics it is also necessary to have some insight into the mind and motives of the artist. Some time ago in a magazine article Mo Jupp said:

> I think today's potters should address themselves to today's problems ... I enjoy using clay more than any other material because I can manipulate it better, I can do what I want. I don't know if I am a sculptor or a potter, it doesn't matter. I try to solve problems.

Those words seem apt for those whose work is described here. They are concerned with current issues and are striving to express themselves in an individual way, described by Marcel Duchamp many years ago as 'the habit of mind we call art'.

It is the nature of art to be unique since it springs from an individual sharing particular perceptions in order that the onlooker may understand aspects of life more clearly. It is personal and particular, with its own integrity, often demanding an effort of understanding. It cannot be created by committee or consensus, and in an age when religions have less meaning, there is a need for pride in creativity and for arts to show humanist values; many of the artists shown here speak of their interest in relics left from previous generations, in layers of meaning as well as their decay and disintegration, and in the eroding geology of the earth.

Changes in societies are reflected in the work they leave behind, and pots, like any other artefact, illustrate development, whether it be technical or ideological. One of the real revolutions of the twentieth century has been in communications, and that is a development likely to go even further during the twenty-first. It is quite possible to create virtual pots on screen – indeed in industry that is already accepted practice – but it is not yet possible for a computer to recreate the tactile pleasure found when handling clay, or the intuitive understanding of material that experience gives.

During the past decades there has been a gradual, if grudging, acceptance of ceramics as a medium for artistic expression, and for those who work with clay to be acknowledged as individual artists rather than anonymous craftsmen. (Women were never previously mentioned.) All those whose work is included here have something to say, and they have chosen unusual methods or materials in which to say it. The relevance of these additions as being integral to the integrity of the piece was one of the criteria used in the difficult decision as to what to include, and what had, regrettably, to be left out. The work could not have been made in any other way.

Another question is then posed: Where do you stop? If only one knew at the beginning what one has discovered by the end! There are many other ceramicists who perhaps should have been mentioned, but there are limitations of time and geography as well as to the numbers of pages or illustrations, and the choice has had to be made from those one knew of, or had heard from and who were willing to participate. There must always be growth and vitality, and since ceramics have demonstrated those qualities for hundreds of years there is every reason to believe they will continue in the same way. However, it is interesting to speculate on what assumptions about our society archaeologists centuries hence will make from the work we leave behind.

'*Dove House*' by Anne Lightwood. Mixed stoneware clays with newsprint pulp, porcelain doves. Once-fired in reduction to 1250°C; unglazed and waxed. The first paperclay piece I made.

Bibliography

Before starting to write the book I read through a great number of ceramics books, but because of the newness of paperclay as a medium for studio potters there is little mention of it. The exception is *Paperclay* by Rosette Gault, published in Britain by A&C Black and in America by University of Pennsylvania Press, Philadelphia.

Colour in Clay by Jane Waller published by The Crowood Press also includes a chapter on paperclay. I cannot imagine being without the regular inspiration and information provided by *Ceramic Review*, published in London by the Craft Potter's Association and read internationally. Other books and publications are listed below.

Books

Andrews, Tim, *Raku* (A&C Black).
Dawson, S. & Turner, S., *A Hand Papermaker's Source Book* (Design Books 1995).
Gregory, Ian, *Kiln Building* (A&C Black).
Gregory, Ian, *Sculptural Ceramics* (A&C Black).
Hamer, Frank and Janet, *The Potter's Dictionary of Materials and Techniques* (A&C Black).
Lane, Peter, *Contemporary Porcelain-Materials, Techniques and Expressions* (A&C Black 1995).
Lane, Peter, *Ceramic Form, Design and Decoration* (A&C Black 1998).
Lane, Peter, *Studio Ceramics* (Collins).
Long, Paulette, *Paper, Art & Technology* (World Print Council 1979).
Norsker, Hendrik, *Clay Materials for the Self-Reliant Potter* (Vieweg 1990).
Scott, Paul, *Ceramics and Print* (A&C Black).
Triplett, Kathy, *Handbuilt Ceramics* (Lark Books, USA).

Magazines

Artists' Newsletter, PO Box 23, Sunderland, SR4 6DG, UK.
Bulletti Informatiu de Ceramica, Sant Honorat 7, Barcelona, Spain.
Ceramics Art and Perception, 35 William Street, Paddington, Sydney NSW 2021, Australia. email: ceramicart@clinipath.com.au
Website http://www.ceramicart.com.au and www.dinamica.it/col/Colman

*P*otter's Dictionary
by Carol Farrow. Fired
book to 1300°C on
earthenware bricks
with enamel glaze.

Ceramics Monthly, 735 Ceramic Place, PO Box 6102, Westerville, Ohio 43086-6102 USA. http://www.ceramicsmonthly.org
Ceramic Review, 21 Carnaby Street, London W1V 1PH, UK. email: ceramic@globalnet. co.uk
Website http://www.ceramic-review.co.uk
Ceramics Technical, address as *Ceramics Art and Perception*.
New Zealand Potter, New Zealand Publications Ltd, PO Box 881, Auckland, NZ.
Pottery in Australia, 48 Burton Street, Darlinghurst, Sydney 2010, Australia.
Revue de la Ceramique et du Verre, 61 Rue Marconi, F-62880, Vendin-le-Viel, France.

All these periodicals include extensive advertisements detailing suppliers of materials and services, with information on new developments and products.

Technical Papers

EKWC: *Fibre Clay* (European Ceramics Work Centre, Hertogenbosch, Holland).

Earths for large-scale design and outdoor low firing. Research Report by Gedula Ogen, Jerusalem, given at International Academy of Ceramics Conference.

Useful Addresses

Paper

Plant Papers, Maureen Richardson, Romilly, Brilley, Hertfordshire, UK
Paper Plus, 24 Zetland Road, Chorlton, Manchester, M21 2TH, UK
The British Paper Co, Frogmore Mill, Hemel Hempstead, Hertfordshire HP3 9RY, UK

Paperclay Materials

MetroSales, Unit 3, 46 Mill Place, Kingston-upon-Thames, Surrey KT1 2RL, UK;
    email: sales@metrosales.co.uk
Paper Clay Products, The Blacksmith's Shop, Pontrilas, Herefordshire HR2 OBB, UK;
    email: michael@paperclay.co.uk; website: http://www.paperclay.co.uk

Fibreglass

Glasplies, 2 Crowland Street, Southport, Lancashire PR9 7RL, UK

Clay Suppliers in UK

Potclays Ltd, Brickkiln Lane, Etruria, Stoke-on-Trent ST4 7BP
W.J. Doble, Newdowns Sand & Clay Pits, St Agnes, Cornwall TR5 OST
The Potter's Connection Ltd, Dept C, Longton Mill, Anchor Road, Longton, Stoke-on-
    Trent, ST3 1JW
Ceramatech Ltd, Frontier Works, 33 Queen Street, London N17 8JA
Potterycrafts, Campbell Road, Stoke-on-Trent, ST4 4ET;
    http://www.potterycrafts.co.uk
Valentine Clay Products, the Sliphouse, Birches Head Road, Hanley, Stoke-on-Trent
    ST1 6LH (suppliers of H.T.G. and Ash White clay mentioned in recipes)
For colours and glaze materials
W.G. Ball Ltd, Longton Mill, Anchor Road, Longton, Stoke-on-Trent, ST3 1JW
Sneyd Oxides Ltd, Sneyd Mills, Leonara Street, Stoke-on-Trent ST6 3BZ

Websites

USA   Craftweb: http://www.craftweb.com
                    www.paperclayart.com
Australia Claynet: http://www.Vicnet.net.au//club/clayhome.htm
Italy   Ceramica on Line: http://www.dinamica.it/
Clayart. email: clayart@Isv.uky.edu
Ceramics and Print. http//www.aber.ac.uk/mov/

The following list was compiled by Graham Hay in 1999, with his comments.
http://art.sdsu.edu/ceramicsweb/ Good search site for discussions on paperclay.
http://www.digitalfire.com/education/clay/paperclay.htm Good no-nonsense introduction.
http://www.ceramicart.com.au/paperclay.htm Articles from *Ceramics Technical*.
http://www.uiah.fi/kll/research/paperclay.hmtl University research on paperclay.
http://www.minidolls.com/techbook/a hazard.htm Hazards and danger of paper, clay and polymer clay.
http://www.paperclayart.com/01rosette.html Rosette Gault's site.

Crofter's Bible by Lotte Glob. Mixed clays, high fired.

Index

There are two sequences: subjects and names. Major references are in **bold** type. Illustrations are indexed under the name of the artist.

SUBJECT INDEX